Northern Wisdom

The Havamal, Tao of the North

Eoghan Odinsson

Visit my website at www.eoghanodinsson.com

Printed in the United States of America

First Printing: February 2012

Typeset in Garamond 12pt

Cover art based on a Photograph of a snowy owl by Fritz Heimerl.

Published by:

 SGARD STUDIOS
Content, Form, Function- Delivered   www.asgard-studios.com

Library and Archives Canada Cataloguing in Publication

Hávamál. English
    Northern wisdom : the Havamal, Tao of the Vikings / [edited by] Eoghan Odinsson.

Includes bibliographical references and index.
ISBN 978-0-9878394-0-4

    1. Old Norse poetry--Translations into English. 2. Mythology, Norse--Poetry--Translations into English. I. Odinsson, Eoghan, 1969- II. Title.

PT7236.A31 2012   839'.61   C2012-900510-X

Foreword

In all the writings of our Northern European ancestors, one source stands head and shoulders above all the others when it comes to practical knowledge on how to live a good life. That work, composed in poetic form in Old Norse, is *the Havamal*. The name translates as The Words of the High One - that is, of Odin, the father of the Nordic gods and the epitome of the wisdom-seeker. In short, this is the advice of a mighty deity: winner of the magical runes, thief of the *Mead of Inspiration*, the one who gave and eye to drink from Mimir's Well of Wisdom. One could hardly ask for a better mentor for a life of success and happiness!

So why have so few people heard of it?

The answers are several: First of all, it's written in a language understandable today only to inhabitants of Iceland and the Faroe Islands north of Scotland, plus a relative handful of specialists. It has been translated into English and other modern languages, of course, but these have all been written by scholars, for scholars. Some versions try to maintain the original poetic meter, at the price of comprehension. Others focus on being absolutely literal, but they, too, use a vocabulary and a phraseology from early medieval times. Without exception, they treat The Words of the High One as a historical document - not as a handbook for life today, in the twenty-first century!

Eoghan Odinsson and his crowdsourcing friends have composed a version of the Havamal that is eminently understandable. No Old Norse poetic forms, no archaic terms, no fuss and no bother. And more than that, this version shows how very relevant this material is! The words of Odin are, as we might expect from a god, every bit as applicable to our lives today as they were a thousand years ago. Good sense is still good sense. We are not so different from our ancestors, after all - we are them recast in a different time and place.

It is my pleasure to write this foreword to Northern Wisdom. I urge you to read it and apply it to your life!

Stephen A. McNallen

Head of the Asatru Folk Assembly - www.runestone.org

Conventions used:

BCE=Before Common Era (aka. BC)
CE=Common Era (aka. AD)

Pronounciation:

- Eth (Ð, ð; also spelled edh or eð) is a letter used in Old English, Icelandic, Faroese (in which it is called edd), and Elfdalian. It was also used in Scandinavia during the Middle Ages, but was subsequently replaced with dh and later d. The capital eth resembles a D with a line partially through the vertical stroke. The lower case resembles an insular d with a line through the top - ð represents a sound like th in English "them".

- Thorn, or þorn (Þ, þ), is a letter in the Old English and Icelandic alphabets, as well as some dialects of Middle English. It was also used in medieval Scandinavia, but was later replaced with the digraph th. The letter originated from the rune Þ in the Elder Fuþark, called thorn in the Anglo-Saxon and thorn or thurs ("giant") in the Scandinavian rune poems, its reconstructed Proto-Germanic name being *Thurisaz. - Þ represents a sound like th in English "thick".

- J in many of the Scandinavaian dialects was pronoucned like a Y, or long I, so you will see words with either a J or I which for the most part represents the same "Yuh' sound.

Also By Eoghan Odinsson

Northern Lore - A Field Guide to the Northern Mind, Body & Spirit (2010)

The Runes in 9 minutes (2012)

Northern Plant Lore - A Field Guide to The Ancestral Use of Plants in Northern Europe (Coming Spring 2012)

Dedication

In memory of a great storyteller and poet, my grandfather,

Hugh Nicholas Long

"Out of the quarrel with others we make rhetoric; out of the quarrel with ourselves we make poetry."

~ W.B. Yeats

Preface

I started this project simply because I wanted a modern language version of the Havamal suitable for easy reading, and also that could be better understood by younger readers. I remember reading an older translation of the Havamal to my son when he was maybe eight years old, and it was a challenge for me to have to explain some of the more antiquated verbiage and turns of phrase; there are also certain metaphors employed that are simply no longer in common usage, and were difficult even for me to decipher.

A second reason was that I wanted to get to know the Havamal better, and try to dig into some of the lessons found there. Although I had read it dozens of times, there were still some verses that I didn't fully understand, and I felt I owed it to my ancestors to spend some time making sure I understood what they were trying to teach me. I confess that I may still not have successfully deciphered every lesson.

Once I made the decision to start the project, the next question was how to go about it? Certainly I could just study the various translations available, but I felt it would be better to work with others, and tap into the collective insight of our folk. Back in my days working in the corporate world there was a technique called "crowdsourcing".

Per Wikipedia: "Crowdsourcing is the act of sourcing tasks traditionally performed by specific individuals to a group of people or community (crowd) through an open call.

Jeff Howe established that the concept of crowdsourcing depends essentially on the fact that because it is an open call to a group of people, it gathers those who are most fit to perform tasks, solve complex problems and contribute with the most relevant and fresh ideas."

This proved to be a very valuable method to re-work the language of the Havamal; not only did it yield a far better result that I would have produced alone, it was great fun! I had the opportunity to share the progress of my work with dozens of other enthusiastic people who contributed many great ideas, and also helped keep me on track when I otherwise might have altered something too much, or perhaps too little.

I primarily used four different translations: **Bellows**, **Bray**, **Chisholm**, and **Hollander**.

Our process was to review the four translations of each verse side by side, and render a verse in plainer language, and that was in keeping with the meaning of the four original translations. I would have preferred to read the original Icelandic and create the modern version directly from my own translation, and in fact I tried that for a couple of weeks, but my command of Old Icelandic was not up to the task. I do plan on creating my own translation as a future project, which will also entail also improving my knowledge of Old Icelandic.

Regarding the number of lines of each verse, originally the Havamal was composed as verse (a poem), and so a certain metre and line scheme was used. The translations that followed did not adhere to the same poetical guidelines, and therefore were not mapped on a line for line basis. I tried when rendering the modern version, to break the verse up such that each line roughly has a piece of meaning, or conveys one part of the verse's message. Sometimes I laid out the modern verse the way it 'felt' right to do so.

Lastly, let me say that I have a deep love of poetry in general, and a special fondness for the lingual patterns of our forefathers; I don't believe I can render the Havamal "better" than some of our great historians and translators did, nor do I think it needs "improving". This is simply a different version for those who might find it useful.

Eoghan Odinsson, 8th day of Yule 2011

Acknowledgements

I would like to thank all my friends on Facebook who participated in the project to review the various translations and who gave me excellent feedback. This truly was a collaborative effort. Here is an incomplete list of some of the regular contributors in no particular order: Mike Lutz, David Heard, Norman Smith, Kaitlyn Gatez, Karl Adolf Andresson, Daniel O'Neil, Shawn Temoin, Cody Charles Carlsson, Robbie Ashmore, Diana L. Driver, Lewen Myers Worell, Adam Lunoe, Ruan Thorgrim Meyer, Darren Hopgood, Mela Helasdottir, Jeremy Paul, Pauline LaBelle, Kyle Sherman, Glen Porterfield, Adre Burger Henning, Robert Anderson, Ellen Keyes, Sean Collins Wright, Andy Erickson. If I missed anyone, I apologize.

And finally, a special thanks goes out to **Steve Charles** who helped enter and update the spreadsheet to compare the various translations – this was a big task, and much appreciated!

As Heimdall had 9 mothers, so did this book come from the efforts of many...
"Heimdal and his Nine Mothers"(1908) by W. G. Collingwood

Contents

INTRODUCTION.. 1

OLD NORTHERN ETHICS FOR LIFE 7

A MODERNIZED HAVAMAL.. 27

WISDOM FOR WANDERERS, ADVICE TO GUESTS 29

Modernized Verse 1 30
Modernized Verse 2 31
Modernized Verse 3 32
Modernized Verse 4 33
Modernized Verse 5 34
Modernized Verse 6 35
Modernized Verse 7 36
Modernized Verse 8 37
Modernized Verse 9 38
Modernized Verse 10 39
Modernized Verse 11 40
Modernized Verse 12 41
Modernized Verse 13 42
Modernized Verse 14 43
Modernized Verse 15 44
Modernized Verse 16 45
Modernized Verse 17 46
Modernized Verse 18 47
Modernized Verse 19 48
Modernized Verse 20 49
Modernized Verse 21 50
Modernized Verse 22 51
Modernized Verse 23 52
Modernized Verse 24 53
Modernized Verse 25 54
Modernized Verse 26 55
Modernized Verse 27 56
Modernized Verse 28 57
Modernized Verse 29 58
Modernized Verse 30 59
Modernized Verse 31 60
Modernized Verse 32 61

Modernized Verse 33 62

Modernized Verse 34 63

Modernized Verse 35 64

Modernized Verse 36 65

Modernized Verse 37 66

Modernized Verse 38 67

Modernized Verse 39 68

Modernized Verse 40 69

Modernized Verse 41 70

Modernized Verse 42 71

Modernized Verse 43 72

Modernized Verse 44 73

Modernized Verse 45 74

Modernized Verse 46 75

Modernized Verse 47 76

Modernized Verse 48 77

Modernized Verse 49 78

Modernized Verse 50 79

Modernized Verse 51 80

Modernized Verse 52 81

Modernized Verse 53 82

Modernized Verse 54 83

Modernized Verse 55 84

Modernized Verse 56 85

Modernized Verse 57 86

Modernized Verse 58 87

Modernized Verse 59 88

Modernized Verse 60 89

Modernized Verse 61 90

Modernized Verse 62 91

Modernized Verse 63 92

Modernized Verse 64 93

Modernized Verse 65 94

Modernized Verse 66 95

Modernized Verse 67 96

MAXIMS FOR MEN 97

Modernized Verse 68 98

Modernized Verse 69 99

Modernized Verse 70 100

Modernized Verse 71 101

Modernized Verse 72 102

Modernized Verse 73 103

Modernized Verse 74 104

Modernized Verse 75 105

Modernized Verse 76 106

Modernized Verse 77 107

Modernized Verse 78 108

Modernized Verse 79 109

Modernized Verse 80 110

Modernized Verse 81 111

Modernized Verse 82 112

Modernized Verse 83 113

Modernized Verse 84 114

Modernized Verse 85 115

Modernized Verse 86 116

Modernized Verse 87 117

Modernized Verse 88 118

Modernized Verse 89 119

Modernized Verse 103 120

LESSONS FOR LOVERS 121

Modernized Verse 90 122

Modernized Verse 91 123

Modernized Verse 92 124

Modernized Verse 93 125

Modernized Verse 94 126

Modernized Verse 95 127

ODIN'S LOVE QUESTS 129

Modernized Verse 96 130

Modernized Verse 97 131

Modernized Verse 98 132

Modernized Verse 99 133

Modernized Verse 100 134

Modernized Verse 101 135

Modernized Verse 102 136

ODIN'S QUEST FOR THE MEAD OF POETRY 137

Modernized Verse 104 138

Modernized Verse 105 139

Modernized Verse 106 140

Modernized Verse 107 141

Modernized Verse 108 142

Modernized Verse 109 143

Modernized Verse 110 144

COUNSELING OF THE STRAY-SINGER 145

Modernized Verse 111 146
Modernized Verse 112 147
Modernized Verse 113 148
Modernized Verse 114 149
Modernized Verse 115 150
Modernized Verse 116 151
Modernized Verse 117 152
Modernized Verse 118 153
Modernized Verse 119 154
Modernized Verse 120 155
Modernized Verse 121 156
Modernized Verse 122 157
Modernized Verse 123 158
Modernized Verse 124 159
Modernized Verse 125 160
Modernized Verse 126 161
Modernized Verse 127 162
Modernized Verse 128 163
Modernized Verse 129 164
Modernized Verse 130 165
Modernized Verse 131 166
Modernized Verse 132 167
Modernized Verse 133 168
Modernized Verse 134 169
Modernized Verse 135 170
Modernized Verse 136 171
Modernized Verse 137 172

A VIKING BOOK OF SPELLS 173

Modernized Verse 138 175
Modernized Verse 139 176
Modernized Verse 140 177
Modernized Verse 141 178
Modernized Verse 142 179
Modernized Verse 143 180
Modernized Verse 144 181
Modernized Verse 145 182
Modernized Verse 146 183
Modernized Verse 147 184
Modernized Verse 148 185
Modernized Verse 149 186
Modernized Verse 150 187
Modernized Verse 151 188
Modernized Verse 152 189

Modernized Verse 153 190
Modernized Verse 154 191
Modernized Verse 155 192
Modernized Verse 156 193
Modernized Verse 157 194
Modernized Verse 158 195
Modernized Verse 159 196
Modernized Verse 160 197
Modernized Verse 161 198
Modernized Verse 162 199
Modernized Verse 163 200
Modernized Verse 164 201
Modernized Verse 165 202

APPENDIX A 203

INDEX 205

BIBLIOGRAPHY 213

Introduction

For nearly thirty years I've been on a personal journey of discovery. As young men do, I started searching for some additional meaning to my existence, that extra layer upon which many believe the best of life is to be found.

What began as an exploration into the realm of the physical, matured into a discovery of the spiritual.

As a boy I was exposed to eastern philosophy through my fascination with the martial arts. Movies starring Bruce Lee, or those classic Samurai films by legendary director Akira Kurosawa, were a powerful enticement for me to sample the eastern arts.

I began with a study of Shotokan Karate, which is a traditional and rugged style. Karate roughly translated in Japanese means "art of the empty hand", and was originally cultivated by Buddhist Monks as an unarmed form of self-defense; later it was adopted by the disarmed peasantry of Japan, which is echoed in the weapons used in many forms of Karate such as the Kama (a sickle), Tonfa (used for beating the chaff from the grain) etc.

I was fortunate to have a teacher, or "Sensei", to use the Japanese term, who had lived and trained in Japan. Through his teaching I was able to get a sense of the sternness, and gravitas of the Japanese culture, which I quite appreciated.

My Sensei always taught restraint, and that Karate was to be used for self-defense only. I still remember being taught the "first rule of self-defense" - run!

My class also cross-trained in other arts, via guest lecturers, in Bo-Jutsu, Iaido and more. I studied with him for a few years before moving on to other pursuits and getting busy with life in general.

After getting married, I decided once again to continue my martial arts training, this time choosing Ju-Jitsu, which is the ancient art of unarmed combat used by the Samurai, and is the foundation for modern sport Judo. It's quite a vicious art, in that it's designed to incapacitate and relies on many joint locks, throws and other lethal strikes. When a Samurai lost his sword, he wasn't worried about lawsuits and jail-time, this was about survival on the battlefield - practicality and pragmatism ruled the day.

A couple of years passed and I switched jobs and there happened to be a Shito-Ryu Karate school around the corner from my office, at which I spent the next several years learning. Shito-Ryu is a form of Karate from the Okinawan Islands (off the southwest coast of Japan). My training at this dojo (place of the way, or school) wasn't much focused on the spiritual aspects, but more on the physical - and it sure was physical! My Black Belt test was conducted over three weekends, each day with something like 6 hours of testing - thousands of push-ups, sit-ups, katas, and drills, followed up by sparring sessions till we wanted to drop; six grueling days of testing. It was a crucible. I finished better for it, knowing that I could will my body to do things I previously thought unimaginable, so in that sense there was a spiritual component, a tempering of the will, and a glimpse into the possible.

In parallel with my physical training, I was also exploring the culture and spiritual offerings of the Far East, starting with Zen Buddhism, a natural compliment to my martial arts training, and then back to general Buddhism. For my part, I felt that Buddhism was a noble and peaceful pursuit, but perhaps too peaceful for what I knew was a world ready to take advantage of that sentiment. Zen seemed to rationalize the violent pursuits of the Samurai and peaceful nature of Buddhism with cryptic puzzles, but my unworldly mind couldn't decipher much of what may have been hidden there.

It was at this point in my life that my career as a consultant in the software industry, and teacher at the University of Aberdeen, had me traveling the world. I spent time wandering the highlands of Scotland where my ancestors had fared, fierce warriors who were known as "The Children of the Mist" - Clan McGregor in Scotland (my mother's people). I also spent time at some of the great historic sites in England and Europe, such as Stonehenge and Sutton-Hoo.

These were places of great power and I truly felt humbled walking the land where my ancestors had lived and died for maybe 10,000 years. My family came to Canada only three generations ago, and is relatively new to North America; my history and family spirit lies deeply rooted in North Western Europe.

As my mother's people were descended from the Highlanders, My father's people were of Viking stock that came to England via the Norman invasion in 1066. The Normans were "Northmen" (Vikings) who "settled" in North Western France; in actuality they were given a large tract of land so they would stop raiding the rest of France.

I was delighted when I started receiving work that sent me to the Far East, and worked in places like India, and Singapore. India is truly an amazing land. There I visited Kanchipuram - nicknamed *"The*

Golden City of 1,000 Temples". I meditated in Hindu temples, rode elephants, ate with my hands, and immersed myself in the land and culture that spawned the Bhagavad-Gita.

> *"In the morning I bathe my intellect in the stupendous and cosmogonal philosophy of the Bhagavad-Gita, in comparison with which our modern world and its literature seems puny and trivial."*

> ~ *Henry David Thoreau*

Hinduism is the most ancient religion and spiritual path in the world, and interestingly, there are many parallels with the Hindu gods and those of the Northern Europeans in Heathen times; Indra and Thor are said to possibly stem from the same Proto-Indo-European deity. Many historians and anthropologists believe our common ancestors migrated from the plains of Eastern Russia and the Ural Mountains, with some folk settling as far south as Northern India, and others continuing on to settle further west in Europe.

No quest for wisdom would be complete without a little Machiavelli, whose very name has given birth to an almost derogatory term, "Machiavellian", which we mean to be synonymous with ruthlessness, cunning, and guile. Niccolò Machiavelli's book *"The Prince"* is really quite practical. For example, if you plan to take over someone's kingdom, he admonishes that you eliminate all the heirs so that nobody comes for revenge later on; sensible, certainly, yet brutal. It occurred to me that playing that kind of "game" those are the rules you need to follow, if you hope to win; certainly not my kind of game, but it's helpful to know how to play.

My search for wisdom and spirituality continued and lead me to what I consider one of the great books on practical living - *The Havamal*. The Havamal is actually a poem, mythologically attributed to Odin, chief of the Norse gods, and written down in Iceland around the 13th century. The Havamal is part of a compilation of poems collectively known as the *"Eddas"* which include much of the material on which our knowledge of the old Heathen gods are based.

The Havamal is a mixture of practical tips for lovers, warfare, advice when travelling and a few magic spells thrown in as well. It's an incredible treasure trove and sampling of our forefather's wisdom.

Like *"The Prince"*, it contains much practical advice in the face of perilous conditions, but unlike Zen, is not couched in riddles; there are some stories that rely on the old Norse concept of Kennings, which assumes you have knowledge of the myths and old ways and uses phrases from them in the place of a single word. For example "Whale Road" means the Sea, "Otter's Bath" might refer to a river. Kennings embellish and beautify the messages, not obfuscate them.

Now that we've traced my path up to the Havamal, I would like to hand the reigns over to someone who can give you the best introduction to the Havamal and its significance in Northern culture - Patrick Lafcadio Hearn.

Patrick Lafcadio Hearn *(1850-1904)*, a man also known by the Japanese name *Koizumi Yakumo*, was an international writer, known best for his books about Japan, especially his collections of Japanese legends and ghost stories, such as *Kwaidan*. In the United States, Hearn is also known for his writings about the city of New Orleans based on his 10-year stay in that city. In 1890 he moved to Japan and later began teaching English Literature at the Tokyo Imperial University. He wrote an essay on the Havamal in order to teach his Japanese students something of the European and English way of being.

I discovered his essay when researching my first book *Northern Lore*, and it's one of my favorite pieces of literature, right up with *Walden* by Henry David Thoreau.

"The Stranger at the Door" (1908) by W. G. Collingwood.

OLD NORTHERN ETHICS FOR LIFE

[Note: This Essay was written circa 1900 by Patrick Lafcadio Hearn, for his Japanese students at the Tokyo Imperial University]

Most of the "Havamal" is a collection of ethical teaching. All that has been preserved by it has been published and translated by Professors Vigfusson and Powell. It is very old—perhaps the oldest Northern literature that we have. I am going to attempt a short lecture upon it, because it is very closely related to the subject of Northern character, and will help us, perhaps better than almost anything else, to understand how the ancestors of the English felt and thought before they became Christians. Nor is this all. I venture to say that the character of the modern English people still retains much more of the quality indicated by the "Havamal" than of the quality implied by Christianity.

The old Northern gods are not dead; they rule a very great part of the world today.

The proverbial philosophy of a people helps us to understand more about them than any other kind of literature. And this sort of literature is certainly among the oldest. It represents only the result of human experience in society, the wisdom that men get by contact with each other, the results of familiarity with right and wrong. By studying the proverbs of a people, you can always make a very good guess as to whether you could live comfortably among them or not.

Froude, in one of his sketches of travel in Norway, made the excellent observation that if -we could suddenly go back to the time of the terrible sea-kings, if we could revisit to-day the homes of the old Northern pirates, and find them exactly as they were one thousand or fifteen hundred years ago, we should find them very much like the modern Englishmen—big, simple, silent men, concealing a great deal of shrewdness under an aspect of simplicity. The teachings of the "Havamal" give great force to this supposition. The book must have been known in some form to the early English—or at least the verses composing it (it is all written in verse) ; and as I have already said, the morals of the old English, as well as their character, differed very little from those of the men of the still further North, with whom they mingled and intermarried freely, both before and after the Danish conquest, when for one moment England and Sweden were one kingdom.

Of course you must remember that Northern society was a very terrible thing in some ways. Every man carried his life in his hands; every farmer kept sword and spear at his side even in his own fields; and every man expected to die fighting. In fact, among the men of the more savage North—the men of Norway in especial—it was considered a great disgrace to die of sickness, to die on one's bed.

That was not to die like a man. Men would go out and get themselves killed, when they felt old age or sickness coming on. But these facts must not blind us to the other fact that there was even in that society a great force of moral cohesion, and sound principles of morality. If there had not been, it could not have existed; much less could the people who lived under it have become the masters of a great part of the world, which they are at the present day. There was, in spite of all that fierceness, much kindness and good nature among them; there were rules of conduct such as no man could find fault with—rules which still govern English society to some extent. And there was opportunity enough for social amusement, social enjoyment, and the winning of public esteem by a noble life.

Still, even in the "Havamal," one is occasionally startled by teachings, which show the darker side of Northern life, a life of perpetual vendetta. As in old Japan, no man could live under the same heaven with the murderer of his brother or father; vengeance was a duty even in the case of a friend. On the subject of enemies the "Havamal" gives not a little curious advice:

> *A man should never step a foot beyond his weapons; for he can never tell where, on his path without, he may need his spear.*

> *A man, before he goes into a house, should look to and espy all the doorways (so that he can find his way out quickly again), for he can never know where foes may be sitting in another man's house.*

Does not this remind us of the Japanese proverb that everybody has three enemies outside of his own door? But the meaning of the "Havamal" teaching is much more sinister. And when the man goes into the house, he is still told to be extremely watchful—to keep his ears and eyes open so that he may not be taken by surprise:

> *The wary guest keeps watchful silence; he listens with his ears and peers about with his eyes; thus does every wise man look about him.*

Northern Wisdom

One would think that men must have had very strong nerves to take comfort under such circumstances, but the poet tells us that the man who can enjoy nothing must be both a coward and a fool. Although a man was to keep watch to protect his life, that was not a reason why he should be afraid of losing it. There were but three things of which a man should be particularly afraid. The first was drink—because drink often caused a man to lose control of his temper; the second was another man's wife—repeatedly the reader is warned never to make love to another man's wife; and the third was thieves—men who would pretend friendship for the purpose of killing and stealing. The man who could keep constant watch over himself and his surroundings was, of course, likely to have the longest life.

Now in all countries there is a great deal of ethical teaching, and always has been, on the subject of speech. The "Havamal" is full of teaching on this subject—the necessity of silence, the danger and the folly of reckless talk. You all know the Japanese proverb that "the mouth is the front gate of all misfortune." The Norse poet puts the same truth into a grimmer shape: "The tongue works death to the head." Here are a number of sayings on this subject:

He that is never silent talks much folly; a glib tongue, unless it be bridled, will often talk a man into trouble.

Do not speak three angry words with a worse man; for often the better man falls by the worse man's sword.

Smile thou in the face of the man thou trustest not, and speak against thy mind.

This is of course a teaching of cunning; but it is the teaching, however immoral, that rules in English society to-day. In the old Norse, however, there were many reasons for having a quarrel whenever possible—reasons which must have existed also in feudal Japan. A man might not care about losing his own life; but he had to be careful not to stir up a feud that might go on for a hundred years. Although there was a great deal of killing, killing always remained a serious matter, because for every killing there had to be a vengeance. It is true that the law exonerated the man who killed another, if he paid a certain blood-price; murder was not legally considered an unpardonable crime. But the family of the dead man would very seldom be satisfied with a payment; they would want blood for blood. Accordingly men had to be very cautious about quarreling, however brave they might personally be.

But all this caution about silence and about watchfulness did not mean that a man should be unable to speak to the purpose when speech was required. "A wise man," says the "Havamal," "should be able both to ask and to answer." There is a proverb which you know, to the effect that you cannot shut the door upon another man's mouth. So says the Norse poet:

"The sons of men can keep silence about nothing that passes among men; therefore a man should be able to take his own part, prudently and strongly."

Says the "Havamal":

"A fool thinks he knows everything if he sits snug in his little corner; but he is at a loss for words if the people put to him a question."

Elsewhere it is said:

"Arch dunce is he who can speak nought, for that is the mark of a fool." And the sum of all this teaching about the tongue is that men should never speak without good reason, and then should speak to the point strongly and wisely.

On the subject of fools there is a great deal in the "Havamal"; but you must understand always by the word fool, in the Northern sense, a man of weak character who knows not what to do in time of difficulty. That was a fool among those men, and a dangerous fool;

for in such a state of society mistakes in act or in speech might reach to terrible consequences. See these little observations about fools:

> *Open-handed, bold-hearted men live most happily, they never feel care; but a fool troubles himself about everything. The niggard pines for gifts.*

> *A fool is awake all night, worrying about everything; when the morning comes he is worn out, and all his troubles are just the same as before.*

> *A fool thinks that all who smile upon him are his friends, not knowing, when he is with wise men, who there may be plotting against him.*

> *If a fool gets a drink, all his mind is immediately displayed.*

But it was not considered right for a man not to drink, although drink was a dangerous thing. On the contrary, not to drink would have been thought a mark of cowardice and of incapacity for self-control. A man was expected even to get drunk if necessary, and to keep his tongue and his temper no matter how much he drank. The strong character would only become more cautious and more silent under the influence of drink; the weak man would immediately show his weakness. I am told the curious fact that in the English army at the present day officers are expected to act very much after the teaching of the old Norse poet; a man is expected to be able on occasion to drink a considerable amount of wine or spirits without showing the effects of it, either in his conduct or in his speech. "Drink thy share of mead; speak fair or not at all"—that was the old text, and a very sensible one in its way.

Laughter was also condemned, if indulged in without very good cause. "The miserable man whose mind is warped laughs at everything, not knowing what he ought to know, that he himself has no lack of faults." I need scarcely tell you that the English are still a very serious people, not disposed to laugh nearly so much as are the men of the more sympathetic Latin races. You will remember perhaps Lord Chesterfield's saying that since he became a man no man had ever seen him laugh. I remember about twenty years ago that there was published by some Englishman a very learned and very interesting little book, called "The Philosophy of Laughter," in which it was gravely asserted that all laughter was foolish. I must acknowledge, however, that no book ever made me laugh more than the volume in question. The great virtue of the men of the North, according to the "Havamal," was indeed the virtue which has given to the English race its present great position among nations,—the simplest of all virtues, common sense. But common sense means much more than the words might imply to the Japanese students, or to any one unfamiliar with English idioms. Common sense, or mother-wit, means natural intelligence, as opposed to, and independent of, cultivated or educated intelligence. It means inherited knowledge; and inherited knowledge may take even the form of genius. It means foresight. It means intuitive knowledge of other people's character. It means cunning as well as broad comprehension. And the modern Englishman, in all times and in all countries, trusts especially to this faculty, which is very largely developed in the race to which he belongs. No Englishman believes in working from book learning. He suspects all theories, philosophical or other. He suspects everything new, and dislikes it, unless he can be compelled by the force of circumstances to see that this new thing has advantages over the old. Race-experience is what he invariably depends upon, whenever he can, whether in India, in Egypt, or in Australia. His statesmen do not consult historical precedents in order to decide what to do: they first learn the facts as they are; then they depend upon their own common sense, not at all upon their university learning or upon philosophical theories. And in the case of the English nation, it must be acknowledged that this instinctive method has been eminently successful. When the "Havamal" speaks of wisdom it means mother-wit, and nothing else; indeed, there was no reading or writing to speak of in those times:

No man can carry better baggage on his journey than wisdom.

There is no better friend than great common sense.

But the wise man should not show himself to be wise without occasion. He should remember that the majority of men are not wise, and he should be careful not to show his superiority over them unnecessarily. Neither should he despise men who do not happen to be as wise as himself:

No man is so good but there is a flaw in him, nor so bad as to be good for nothing.

Middling wise should every man be; never overwise. Those who know many things rarely lead the happiest life.

Middling wise should every man be; never overwise. No man should know his fate beforehand; so shall he live freest from care.

Middling wise should every man be, never too wise. A wise man's heart is seldom glad, if its owner be a true sage.

This is the ancient wisdom also of Solomon: "He that increases wisdom increases sorrow." But how very true as worldly wisdom these little Northern sentences are. That a man who knows a little of many things, and no one thing perfectly, is the happiest man—this certainly is even more true to-day than it was a thousand years ago. Spencer has well observed that the man who can influence his generation, is never the man greatly in advance of his time, but only the man who is very slightly better than his fellows. The man who is very superior is likely to be ignored or disliked. Mediocrity can not help disliking superiority; and as the old Northern sage declared, "the average of men is but moiety." Moiety does not mean necessarily mediocrity, but also that which is below mediocrity. What we call in

England to-day, as Matthew Arnold called it, the Philistine element, continues to prove in our own time, to almost every superior man, the danger of being too wise.

Interesting in another way, and altogether more agreeable, are the old sayings about friendship: "Know this, if thou hast a trusty friend, go and see him often; because a road which is seldom trod gets choked with brambles and high grass."

> *Be not thou the first to break off from thy friend. Sorrow will eat thy heart if thou lackest the friend to open thy heart to.*

> *Anything is better than to be false; he is no friend who only speaks to please.*

Which means, of course, that a true friend is not afraid to find fault with his friend's course; indeed, that is his solemn duty. But these teachings about friendship are accompanied with many cautions; for one must be very careful in the making of friends. The ancient Greeks had a terrible proverb:

> *"Treat your friend as if he should become some day your enemy; and treat your enemy as if he might some day become your friend."*

This proverb seems to me to indicate a certain amount of doubt in human nature. We do not find this doubt in the Norse teaching, but on the contrary, some very excellent advice. The first thing to remember is that friendship is sacred: "He that opens his heart to another mixes blood with him." Therefore one should be very careful either about forming or about breaking a friendship.

> *A man should be a friend to his friend's friend. But no man should be a friend of his friend's foe, nor of his foe's friend.*

> *A man should be a friend with his friend, and pay back gift with gift; give back laughter for laughter (to his enemies), and lesing for lies.*

Give and give back makes the longest friend. Give not overmuch at one time. Gift always looks for return.

The poet also tells us how trifling gifts are quite sufficient to make friends and to keep them, if wisely given. A costly gift may seem like a bribe; a little gift is only the sign of kindly feeling. And as a mere matter of justice, a costly gift may be unkind, for it puts the friend under an obligation which he may not be rich enough to repay. Repeatedly we are told also that too much should not be expected of friendship. The value of a friend is his affection, his sympathy; but favours that cost must always be returned.

I never met a man so open-hearted and free with his food, but that boon was boon to him—nor so generous as not to look for return if he had a chance.

Emerson says almost precisely the same thing in his essay on friendship—showing how little human wisdom has changed in all the centuries. Here is another good bit of advice concerning visits:

It is far away to an ill friend, even though he live on one's road; but to a good friend there is a short cut, even though he live far out.

Go on, be not a guest ever in the same house. The welcome becomes wearisome if he sits too long at another's table.

This means that we must not impose on our friends; but there is a further caution on the subject of eating at a friend's house. You must not go to your friend's house hungry, when you can help it.

A man should take his meal betimes, before he goes to his neighbour—or he will sit and seem hungered like one starving, and have no power to talk.

That is the main point to remember in dining at another's house, that you are not there only for your own pleasure, but for that of other people. You are expected to talk; and you cannot talk if you are very hungry. At this very day a gentleman makes it the rule to do the same thing. Accordingly we see that these rough men of the North must have had a good deal of social refinement—refinement not of dress or of speech, but of feeling. Still, says the poet, one's own home is the best, though it be but a cottage. "A man is a man in his own house."

Now we come to some sentences teaching caution, which are noteworthy in a certain way:

> *Tell one man thy secret, but not two. What three men know, all the world knows.*

> *Never let a bad man know thy mishaps; for from a bad man thou shalt never get reward for thy sincerity.*

I shall presently give you some modern examples in regard to the advice concerning bad men. Another thing to be cautious about is praise. If you have to be careful about blame, you must be very cautious also about praise.

> *Praise the day at even-tide; a woman at her burying; a sword when it has been tried; a maid when she is married; ice when you have crossed over it; ale when it is drunk.*

If there is anything noteworthy in English character to-day it is the exemplification of this very kind of teaching. This is essentially Northern. The last people from whom praise can be expected, even for what is worthy of all praise, are the English. A new friendship, a new ideal, a reform, a noble action, a wonderful poet, an exquisite painting—any of these things will be admired and praised by every other people in Europe long before you can get Englishmen to praise. The Englishman all this time is studying, considering, trying to find fault. Why should he try to find fault? So that he will not make any mistakes at a later day. He has inherited the terrible caution of his ancestors in regard to mistakes. It must be granted that his caution has saved him from a number of very serious mistakes that other nations have made. It must also be acknowledged that he exercises a fair amount of moderation in the opposite direction—this modern Englishman; he has learned caution of another kind, which his ancestors taught him. "Power," says the "Havamal," "should be used with moderation; for whoever finds himself among valiant men will discover that no man is peerless." And this is a very important thing for the strong man to know—that however strong, he can not be the strongest; his match will be found when occasion demands it. Not only Scandinavian but English rulers have often discovered this fact to their cost. Another matter to be very anxious about is public opinion.

> *Chattels die; kinsmen pass away; one dies oneself; but I know something that never dies—the name of the man, for good or bad.*

Do not think that this means anything religious. It means only that the reputation of a man goes to influence the good or ill fortune of his descendants. It is something to be proud of, to be the son of a good man; it helps to success in life. On the other hand, to have had a father of ill reputation is a very serious obstacle to success of any kind in countries where the influence of heredity is strongly recognized.

I have nearly exhausted the examples of this Northern wisdom which I selected for you; but there are two subjects which remain to be considered. One is the law of conduct in regard to misfortune; and the other is the rule of conduct in regard to women. A man was expected to keep up a brave heart under any circumstances. These old Northmen seldom committed suicide; and I must tell you that all the talk about Christianity having checked the practice of suicide to some extent, cannot be fairly accepted as truth. In modern England to-day the suicides average nearly three thousand a year; but making allowances for extraordinary circumstances, it is certain that the Northern races consider suicide in an entirely different way from what the Latin races do. There was very little suicide among the men of the North, because every man considered it his duty to get killed, not to kill himself; and to kill himself would have seemed cowardly, as implying fear of being killed by others. In modern ethical training, quite apart from religious considerations, a man is taught that suicide is only excusable in case of shame, or under such exceptional circumstances as have occurred in the history of the Indian mutiny. At all events, we have the feeling still strongly manifested in England that suicide is not quite manly; and this is certainly due much more to ancestral habits of thinking, which date back to pagan days, than to Christian doctrine. As I have said, the pagan English would not commit suicide to escape mere pain. But the Northern people knew how to die to escape shame. There is an awful story in Roman history about the wives and daughters of the conquered German tribes, thousands in number, asking to be promised that their virtue should be respected, and all killing themselves when the Roman general refused the request. No Southern people of Europe in that time would have shown such heroism upon such a matter. Leaving honour aside, however, the old book tells us that a man should never despair.

> *Fire, the sight of the sun, good health, and a blameless life,—these are the goodliest things in this world.*

> *Yet a man is not utterly wretched, though he have bad health, or be maimed.*

> *The halt may ride a horse; the handless may drive a herd; the deaf can fight and do well; better be blind than buried. A corpse is good for naught.*

On the subject of women there is not very much in the book beyond the usual caution in regard to wicked women; but there is this little observation:

Northern Wisdom

Never blame a woman for what is all man's weakness. Hues charming and fair may move the wise and not the dullard. Mighty love turns the son of men from wise to fool.

This is shrewd, and it contains a very remarkable bit of esthetic truth, that it requires a wise man to see certain kinds of beauty, which a stupid man could never be made to understand. And, leaving aside the subject of love, what very good advice it is never to laugh at a person for what can be considered a common failure. In the same way an intelligent man should learn to be patient with the unintelligent, as the same poem elsewhere insists.

Now what is the general result of this little study, the general impression that it leaves upon the mind? Certainly we feel that the life reflected in these sentences was a life in which caution was above all things necessary—caution in thought and speech and act, never ceasing, by night or day, during the whole of a man's life. Caution implies moderation. Moderation inevitably develops a certain habit of justice—a justice that might not extend outside of the race, but a justice that would be exercised between man and man of the same blood. Very much of English character and of English history is explained by the life that the "Havamal" portrays. Very much that is good; also very much that is bad—not bad in one sense, so far as the future of the race is concerned, but in a social way certainly not good. The judgment of the Englishman by all other European peoples is that he is the most suspicious, the most reserved, the most unreceptive, the most unfriendly, the coldest hearted, and the most domineering of all Western peoples. Ask a Frenchman, an Italian, a German, a Spaniard, even an American, what he thinks about Englishmen; and every one of them will tell you the very same thing. This is precisely what the character of men would become who had lived for thousands of years in the conditions of Northern society. But you would find upon the other hand that nearly all nations would speak highly of certain other English qualities—energy, courage, honour, justice (between themselves). They would say that although no man is so difficult to make friends with, the friendship of an

Englishman once gained is more strong and true than any other. And as the battle of life still continues, and must continue for thousands of years to come, it must be acknowledged that the English character is especially well fitted for the struggle. Its reserves, its cautions, its doubts, its suspicions, its brutality—these have been for it in the past, and are still in the present, the best social armour and panoply of war. It is not a lovable nor an amiable character; it is not even kindly. The Englishman of the best type is much more inclined to be just than he is to be kind, for kindness is an emotional impulse, and the Englishman is on his guard against every kind of emotional impulse. But with all this, the character is a grand one, and its success has been the best proof of its value.

Now you will have observed in the reading of this ancient code of social morals that, while none of the teaching is religious, some of it is absolutely immoral from any religious standpoint. No great religion permits us to speak what is not true, and to smile in the face of an enemy while pretending to be his friend. No religion teaches that we should "pay back lies for lies." Neither does a religion tell us that we should expect a return for every kindness done; that we should regard friendship as being actuated by selfish motives; that we should never praise when praise seems to be deserved. In fact, when Sir Walter Scott long ago made a partial translation of the "Havamal," he thought himself obliged to leave out a number of sentences, which seemed to him highly immoral, and to apologize for others. He thought that they would shock English readers too much.

We are not quite so squeamish to-day; and a thinker of our own time would scarcely deny that English society is very largely governed at this moment by the same kind of rules that Sir Walter Scott thought to be so bad. But here we need not condemn English society in particular. All European society has been for hundreds of years conducting itself upon very much the same principles; for the reason that human social experience has been the same in all Western countries. I should say that the only difference between English society and other societies is that the hardness of character is very much greater. Let us go back even to the most Christian times of Western societies in the most Christian country of Europe, and observe whether the social code was then and there so very different from the social code of the old "Havamal." Mr. Spencer observes in his "Ethics" that, so far as the conduct of life is concerned, religion is almost nothing and practice is everything. We find this wonderfully exemplified in a most remarkable book of social precepts written in the seventeenth century, in Spain, under the title of the "Oraculo Manual." It was composed by a Spanish priest, named Baltasar Gracian, who was born in the year 1601 and died in 1658; and it has been translated into nearly all languages. The best English translation, published by Macmillan, is called "The Art of Worldly Wisdom." It is even more admired to-day than in the seventeenth century; and what it teaches as to social conduct holds as good to-day of modern society as it did of society two hundred years ago. It is one of the most unpleasant and yet interesting books ever published— unpleasant because of the malicious cunning which it often displays—interesting because of the frightful perspicacity of the author. The man who wrote that book understood the hearts of men, especially the bad side. He was a gentleman of high rank before he became a priest, and his instinctive shrewdness must have been hereditary. Religion, this man would have said, teaches the best possible morals; but the world is not governed by religion altogether, and to mix with it, we must act according to its dictates.

These dictates remind us in many ways of the cautions and the cunning of the "Havamal." The first thing enjoined upon a man both by the Norse writer and by the Spanish author is the art of silence. Probably this has been the result of social experience in all countries. "Cautious silence is the holy of holies of worldly wisdom," says

Gracian. And he gives many elaborate reasons for this statement, not the least of which is the following: "If you do not declare yourself immediately, you arouse expectation, especially when the importance of your position makes you the object of general attention. Mix a little mystery with everything, and the very mystery arouses veneration." A little further on he gives us exactly the same advice as did the "Havamal" writer, in regard to being frank with enemies. "Do not," he says, "show your wounded finger, for everything will knock up against it; nor complain about it, for malice always aims where weakness can be injured. . . . Never disclose the source of mortification or of joy, if you wish the one to cease, the other to endure." About secrets the Spaniard is quite as cautious as the Norseman. He says, "Especially dangerous are secrets entrusted to friends. He that communicates his secret to another makes himself that other man's slave." But after a great many such cautions in regard to silence and secrecy, he tells us also that we must learn how to fight with the world. You remember the advice of the "Havamal" on this subject, how it condemns as a fool the man who can not answer a reproach. The Spaniard is, however, much more malicious in his suggestions. He tells us that we must "learn to know every man's thumbscrew." I suppose you know that a thumbscrew was an instrument of torture used in old times to force confessions from criminals. This advice means nothing less than that we should learn how to be able to hurt other men's feelings, or to flatter other men's weaknesses. "First guess every man's ruling passion, appeal to it by a word, set it in motion by temptation, and you will infallibly give checkmate to his freedom of will." The term "give checkmate" is taken from the game of chess, and must here be understood as meaning to overcome, to conquer. A kindred piece of advice is "keep a store of sarcasms, and know how to use them." Indeed he tells us that this is the point of greatest tact in human intercourse. "Struck by the slightest word of this kind, many fall away from the closest intimacy with superiors or inferiors, which intimacy could not be in the slightest shaken by a whole conspiracy of popular insinuation or private malevolence." In other words, you can more quickly destroy a man's friendship by one word of sarcasm than by any amount of intrigue. Does not this read very much like sheer wickedness? Certainly it does; but the author would have told you that you must fight the wicked with their own weapons. In the "Havamal" you will not find anything quite so openly wicked as that; but we must suppose that the Norsemen knew the secret, though they might not have put it into words. As for the social teaching, you will find it very subtly expressed even in the modern English novels of George Meredith, who, by the way, has written a poem in praise of sarcasm and ridicule. But let us now see what the Spanish author has to tell us about friendship and unselfishness.

The shrewd man knows that others when they seek him do not seek "him," but "their advantage in him and by him." That is to say, a shrewd man does not believe in disinterested friendship. This is much worse than anything in the "Havamal." And it is diabolically elaborated. What are we to say about such teaching as the following: "A wise man would rather see men needing him than thanking him. To keep them on the threshold of hope is diplomatic; to trust to their gratitude is boorish; hope has a good memory, gratitude a bad one"? There is much more of this kind; but after the assurance that only a boorish person (that is to say, an ignorant and vulgar man) can believe in gratitude, the author's opinion of human nature needs no further elucidation. The old Norseman would have been shocked at such a statement. But he might have approved the following: "When you hear anything favourable, keep a tight rein upon your credulity; if unfavourable, give it the spur." That is to say, when you hear anything good about another man, do not be ready to believe it; but if you hear anything bad about him, believe as much of it as you can.

I notice also many other points of resemblance between the Northern and the Spanish teaching in regard to caution. The "Havamal" says that you must not pick a quarrel with a worse man than yourself; "because the better man often falls by the worse man's sword." The Spanish priest gives a still shrewder reason for the same policy. "Never contend," he says, "with a man who has nothing to lose; for thereby you enter into an unequal conflict. The other enters without anxiety; having lost everything, including shame, he has no further loss to fear." I think that this is an immoral teaching, though a very prudent one; but I need scarcely to tell you that it is still a principle in modern society not to contend with a man who has no reputation to lose. I think it is immoral, because it is purely selfish, and because a good man ought not to be afraid to denounce a wrong because of making enemies. Another point, however, on which the "Havamal" and the priest agree, is more commendable and interesting. "We do not think much of a man who never contradicts us; that is no sign he loves us, but rather a sign that he loves himself. Original and out-of-the way views are signs of superior ability."

I should not like you to suppose, however, that the whole of the book from which I have been quoting is of the same character as the quotations. There is excellent advice in it; and much kindly teaching on the subject of generous acts. It is a book both good and bad, and never stupid. The same man who tells you that friendship is seldom unselfish, also declares that life would be a desert without friends, and that there is no magic like a good turn—that is, a kind act. He teaches the importance of getting good will by honest means, although he advises us also to learn how to injure. I am sure that nobody could read the book without benefit. And I may close these quotations from it with the following paragraph, which is the very best bit of counsel that could be given to a literary student:

Be slow and sure. Quickly done can be quickly undone. To last an eternity requires an eternity of preparation. Only excellence counts. Profound intelligence is the only foundation for immortality. Worth much costs much. The precious metals are the heaviest.

But so far as the question of human conduct is concerned, the book of Gracian is no more of a religious book than is the "Havamal" of the heathen North. You would find, were such a book published to-day and brought up to the present time by any shrewd writer, that Western morality has not improved in the least since the time before Christianity was established, so far as the rules of society go. Society is not, and can not be, religious, because it is a state of continual warfare. Every person in it has to fight, and the battle is not less cruel now because it is not fought with swords. Indeed, I should think that the time when every man carried his sword in society was a time when men were quite as kindly and much more honest than they are now.

The object of this little lecture was to show you that the principles of the ancient Norse are really the principles ruling English society to-day; but I think you will be able to take from it a still larger meaning. It is that not only one form of society, but all forms of society, represent the warfare of man and man. That is why thinkers, poets, philosophers, in all ages, have tried to find solitude, to keep out of the contest, to devote themselves only to study of the beautiful and the true. But the prizes of life are not to be obtained in solitude, although the prizes of thought can only there be won. After all, whatever we may think about the cruelty and treachery of the social world, it does great things in the end. It quickens judgment, deepens intelligence, enforces the acquisition of self-control, creates forms of mental and moral strength that cannot fail to be sometimes of vast importance to mankind. But if you should ask me whether it increases human happiness, I should certainly say "no." The "Havamal" said the same thing:

The truly wise man cannot be happy.

Patrick Lafcadio Hearn

A Modernized Havamal

The Following is the Havamal in slightly more modern language. The "Old Verse" presented on each page is Henry Adam Bellows' translation. I've also add some "Keywords" which are just a handy guide when studying the Havamal.

Where necessary I've included notes to help the reader understand the decisions we made when modernizing a particular verse, word or phrase. If you see something you believe needs to be changed, please e-mail me at havamal@eoghanodinsson.com and I'll be sure to include any required changes in the next version.

The Havamal is comprised of distinct sections aimed at educating the reader on different topics.

Northern Wisdom

Professor D.L. Ashliman, retired from the University of Pittsburgh, still maintains a page[1] on the web that has Olive Bray's translation of the Havamal organized by eight categories.

I've followed his example but renamed the categories slightly and moved a few of the verses into different categories to align more closely with the other translations of the Havamal:

1. Wisdom for Wanderers, Advice to Guests (verses 1-67)
2. Maxims for Men (verses 68-89 & 103)
3. Lessons for Lovers (verses 90-95)
4. Odin's Love Quests (verses 96-102, 104-110)
5. Odin's Quest for the Mead of Poetry (verses 111-137)
6. The Counseling of the Stray-Singer (verses 138-136)
7. Odin's Quest for the Runes (verses 137-145)
8. The Song of Spells (verses 146-165)

---

[1] http://www.pitt.edu/~dash/havamal.html

Wisdom for Wanderers, Advice to Guests

Modernized Verse 1

Before passing through any door,

Observe carefully,

and consider what may be ahead.

Always be mindful of your surroundings,

Be vigilant in unfamiliar places.

You can never be sure where a foe,

Or other danger resides.

Keywords:

Vigilance, Awareness, Caution

OLD VERSE 1

Within the gates, ere a man shall go,

Full warily let him watch,

Full long let him look about him;

For little he knows, where a foe may lurk,

And sit in the seats within.

Modernized Verse 2

Hail to the Host!

A guest has arrived.

Are you prepared,

to give him a place to rest?

A weary traveler may be impatient,

for warmth and kindness.

Keywords:

Hospitality, Promptness

OLD VERSE 2

hail to the giver! A guest has come;
Where shall the stranger sit?
Swift shall he be who, with swords shall try
The proof of his might to make.

Modernized Verse 3

A traveler or guest,

seeking your hospitality,

may be cold and weary.

Who knows what hardships,

on his journey he endured?

Keywords:

Concern, Compassion

OLD VERSE 3

Fire he needs, who with frozen knees

has come from the cold without:

Food and clothes, must the farer have,

The man from the mountains come.

Modernized Verse 4

A guest may need drink and food,

perhaps fresh clothing,

and kind words.

Make your guest comfortable,

ensure he knows he is welcome

to come again.

Keywords:

Graciousness, Welcoming

OLD VERSE 4

Water and towels, and welcoming speech
Should he find who comes, to the feast;
If renown he would get, and again be greeted,
Wisely and well must he act.

Modernized Verse 5

If you plan to travel,

have your wits about you.

Pay attention,

the unwise should stay at home.

You will be considered a fool and mocked,

if you can't speak intelligently with other men.

Keywords:

Alertness, General Knowledge, Worldliness

OLD VERSE 5

Wits must he have, who wanders wide,
But all is easy at home;
At the witless man, the wise shall wink
When among such men he sits.

Modernized Verse 6

Let a man not be boastful about his wisdom,

but watchful instead.

The wise and silent rarely get into trouble,

when in the company of others.

A more trustworthy friend,

a man cannot have, than understanding.

Keywords:

Wisdom, Caution, Understanding

OLD VERSE 6

A man shall not boast, of his keenness of mind,

But keep it close in his breast;

To the silent and wise, does ill come seldom

When he goes as guest to a house;

For a faster friend one never finds

Than wisdom tried and true.

Modernized Verse 7

The cautious guest,

who goes to a gathering with strangers,

keeps his eyes and ears open,

and his mouth closed.

Much wisdom can be gained,

from quiet observation.

Keywords:

Alertness, Quiet Observation

OLD VERSE 7

The knowing guest, who goes to the feast,
In silent attention sits;
With his ears he hears, with his eyes he watches,
Thus wary are wise men all.

Modernized Verse 8

It's a fortunate man,

who is well respected by others,

for the deeds he has done himself.

It's more difficult if you rely on others,

to help make your good reputation.

Keywords:

Accomplishment, Self-Reliance

OLD VERSE 8

happy the one, who wins for himself

favor and praises fair;

Less safe by far, is the wisdom found

That is hid in another's heart.

Modernized Verse 9

It's good to be well respected while you live,

and to be able to think for yourself.

Men often give each other bad advice.

Keywords:

Respect, Independent Thinking, Bad Advice

OLD VERSE 9

happy the man, who has while he lives

Wisdom and praise as well,

For evil counsel, a man full oft

has from another's heart.

Modernized Verse 10

There is nothing better,

that a man may possess,

than a little common sense.

It's better than being rich,

especially in strange places and new situations.

This is the poor man's real wealth.

Keywords:

New Situations, Common Sense, True Wealth

OLD VERSE 10

A better burden, may no man bear
For wanderings wide than wisdom:
It is better than wealth, on unknown ways,
And in grief a refuge it gives.

Modernized Verse 11

There is nothing better

that a man may possess,

than a little common sense.

Whether you are traveling,

or encumbered by too much alcohol,

good sense is the best tool you have to keep you safe.

Keywords:

Travel, Drunkenness, Common Sense, Best Tool

OLD VERSE 11

A better burden may no man bear,

For wanderings wide than wisdom;

Worse food for the journey he brings not afield

Than an over-drinking of ale.

Modernized Verse 12

Too much alcohol is not a good thing,

although some may tell you otherwise

The more you drink,

the less you know.

Keywords:

Alcohol, Moderation, Self-Control

OLD VERSE 12

Less good there lies, than most believe,
In ale for mortal men;
For the more he drinks the less does man,
Of his mind the mastery hold.

Modernized Verse 13

Forgetfulness hovers like a heron[2],

where you drink too much.

It robs a man of his mind and good sense.

One night at Gunnlöð's[3] place,

this happened to me.

Keywords:

Drunkenness, Forgetfulness

OLD VERSE 13

Over beer the bird of forgetfulness broods,
And steals the minds of men;
With the heron's feathers fettered I lay
And in Gunnloth's house was held.

---

[2] The Heron symbolizes a quiet persistence, it stands for hours never moving. The lesson here is that when you drink too much, you have a fog over your mind that hovers persistently like a Heron.

[3] Gunnlöð is daughter of the giant Suttungr, who set her to guard the mead of poetry. Gunnlöð was seduced by Odin, who according to the Prose Edda bargained three nights of sex for three sips of the mead and then tricked her, stealing all of it.

Modernized Verse 14

I became far too drunk,

at the wise Fjalar's gathering.

The best party is one where

you drink in moderation

and keep your wits.

Keywords:

Alcohol, Moderation, Accountability

OLD VERSE 14

Drunk I was, I was dead-drunk,

When with Fjalar wise I was; '

Tis the best of drinking

if back one brings his wisdom with him home.

Modernized Verse 15

A leader should listen to his followers,

be charitable,

and show courage in times of trouble.

All a man's life he should strive to have a positive outlook,

and always be ready to contribute and do his part.

Keywords:

Charity, Courage, Optimism, Readiness

OLD VERSE 15

The son of a king shall be silent and wise,

And bold in battle as well;

Bravely and gladly a man shall go,

Till the day of his death is come.

Modernized Verse 16

The coward thinks he will live forever,

by avoiding battle and other dangers.

Old age spares no man,

despite escaping harm.

Keywords:

Cowardice, Fate

OLD VERSE 16

The sluggard believes he shall live forever,
If the fight he faces not;
But age shall not grant him the gift of peace,
Though spears may spare his life.

Modernized Verse 17

A foolish man gapes,

when at a party with friends or family.

He prattles, mopes and stares,

the whole time.

If he drinks a little,

he becomes more comfortable and at ease.

Keywords:

Shy Fool, Social Drinking

OLD VERSE 17

The fool is agape when he comes to the feast,
he stammers or else is still;
But soon if he gets a drink is it seen
What the mind of the man is like.

Modernized Verse 18

A man's perception of others,

grows the more places he visits,

and the wider he's traveled.

The wise man,

begins to understand,

what motivates other men.

Keywords:

Worldliness, Understanding

OLD VERSE 18

he alone is aware who has wandered wide,

And far abroad has fared,

how great a mind is guided by him

That wealth of wisdom has.

Modernized Verse 19

You don't need to refrain from ever drinking[4],

but when you do, drink in moderation.

If you have something worth saying, then say it,

otherwise it's best to keep quiet.

Don't worry about leaving a party early,

nobody will ridicule you for turning in at a decent hour.

Keywords:

Social Drinking, Speak Sensibly, Retire Early

OLD VERSE

Shun not the mead,

but drink in measure:

Speak to the point or be still:

For rudeness none shall rightly blame thee

If soon thy bed thou seekest.

---

[4] As Hearn says in his essay: "..it was not considered right for a man not to drink, although drink was a dangerous thing. On the contrary, not to drink would have been thought a mark of cowardice and of incapacity for self-control. A man was expected even to get drunk if necessary, and to keep his tongue and his temper no matter how much he drank. The strong character would only become more cautious and more silent under the influence of drink; the weak man would immediately show his weakness.

Modernized Verse 20

The greedy man eats too much.

Among more sensible people,

he's teased and mocked,

for his big belly.

Keywords:

Gluttony

OLD VERSE

The greedy man,
if his mind be vague,
Will eat till sick he is;
The vulgar man,
when among the wise,
To scorn by his belly is brought.

Modernized Verse 21

Even a herd of cows,

stop grazing when they're full.

The glutton never knows,

when to stop eating.

Keywords:

Self-Control

OLD VERSE

The herds know well when home they shall fare,

And then from the grass they go:

But the foolish man his belly's measure

Shall never know aright.

Modernized Verse 22

It's a petty fool,

who laughs at others for their shortcomings.

Nobody is free from faults.

Keywords:

Imperfection

OLD VERSE

A paltry man and poor of mind,

At all things ever mocks;

For never he knows, what he ought to know,

That he is not free from faults.

Modernized Verse 23

It does no good to lie awake all night,

ruminating on your problems.

You wake up tired,

and your troubles are still there.

Keywords:

Obsessing, Worry

OLD VERSE

The witless man is awake all night,

Thinking of many things;

Care-worn he is when the morning comes,

And his woe is just as it was.

Modernized Verse 24

The fool thinks,

all who laugh with him are friends.

He doesn't understand,

wiser men are laughing at him.

Keywords:

Foolishness, Misplaced Trust

OLD VERSE

The foolish man for friends all those
Who laugh at him will hold;
When among the wise he marks it not
Though hatred of him they speak.

Modernized Verse 25

The fool thinks,

all who laugh with him are friends.

Then he finds in times of need,

none of those men will help him.

Keywords:

Guile, Abandonment

OLD VERSE

The foolish man for friends all those
Who laugh at him will hold;
But the truth when he comes to the council he learns,
That few in his favor will speak.

Modernized Verse 26

The ignorant fool thinks he knows everything,

when he's safe at home;

He finds he doesn't have much to say,

when questioned by other men.

Keywords:

Overconfidence, Ignorance

OLD VERSE

An ignorant man thinks that all he knows,

When he sits by himself in a corner;

But never what answer to make he knows,

When others with questions come.

Modernized Verse 27

When mingling with others,

a man who knows little is best to be silent.

Nobody will know he's a fool,

unless he opens his mouth.

Keywords:

Reservedness, Caution, Guardedness

OLD VERSE

A witless man,

when he meets with men,

had best in silence abide;

For no one shall find that nothing he knows,

If his mouth is not open too much.

But a man knows not,

if nothing he knows,

When his mouth has been open too much.

Modernized Verse 28

A wise man knows,

how to ask and answer questions intelligently.

Just remember that whatever is said among men,

is difficult to conceal or keep secret from others.

Keywords:

Knowledgeable Discourse, Secrets

OLD VERSE

Wise shall he seem who well can question,

And also answer well;

Nought is concealed that men may say

Among the sons of men.

Modernized Verse 29

Someone who talks non-stop,

isn't going to win many friends.

Unrestrained blabbering,

can get you into a lot of trouble.

Keywords:

Long-Winded, Unwelcome, Dangerous

OLD VERSE

Often he speaks who never is still,

With words that win no faith:

The babbling tongue,

if a bridle it find not,

Oft for itself sings ill.

Modernized Verse 30

Don't ridicule another man,

even if he's a friend or family.

Anyone can seem confident,

if they're not the one in the spotlight.

Keywords:

Ridicule, Cockiness

OLD VERSE

In mockery no one a man shall hold,

Although he fare to the feast;

Wise seems one oft,

if nought he is asked,

And safely he sits dry-skinned.

Modernized Verse 31

The wise man leaves the party,

when people start arguing or slinging insults.

You never know who has enemies,

and what trouble might then ensue.

Keywords:

Precaution, Foresight

OLD VERSE

Wise a guest holds it to take to his heels,

When mock of another he makes;

But little he knows who laughs at the feast,

Though he mocks in the midst of his foes.

Modernized Verse 32

Often people tease each other,

although they might not mean any real harm,

such casual insults,

may lead to bitter anger.

Keywords:

Casual Insults, Consequences

OLD VERSE

Often people tease each other,

although they might not mean any real harm,

such casual insults,

may lead to bitter anger.

Modernized Verse 33

It's a good idea to have something to eat,

before you go to visit friends.

That way you can focus on conversation,

and not preoccupied satisfying your hunger.

Keywords:

Preparation, Priorities

OLD VERSE

Oft should one make an early meal,

Nor fasting come to the feast:

Else he sits and chews as if he would choke,

And little is able to ask.

Modernized Verse 34

It seems like a long and arduous journey

to visit a person you don't like,

even though he might live next door.

But it's always a pleasure to go and visit a true friend,

even if he's half a world away.

Keywords:

Relativity

OLD VERSE

Crooked and far is the road to a foe,

Though his house on the highway be;

But wide and straight is the way to a friend,

Though far away he fare.

Modernized Verse 35

Don't outstay your welcome,

when visiting friends or family.

You risk going from someone who is admired,

to someone who is loathed and despised.

Keywords:

Timing, Self-Awareness, Empathy

OLD VERSE 35

Forth shall one go,

nor stay as a guest

In a single spot forever;

Love becomes loathing if long one sits

By the hearth in another's home.

Modernized Verse 36

Even a little shack of your own is better than none,

at least in your own home you're the master.

Being able to provide for your own needs,

is better than begging in the street.

Keywords:

Independence, Self-Reliance

OLD VERSE 35

Better a house,

though a hut it be,

A man is master at home;

A pair of goats and a patched—up roof

Are better far than begging.

Modernized Verse 37

Even a little shack of your own is better than none,

at least in your own home you're the master.

A man who has to beg for his meals,

is sure to feel discouraged and heartsick.

Keywords:

Self-Reliance, Dependence

OLD VERSE 37

Better a house,

though a hut it be,

A man is master at home;

his heart is bleeding who needs must beg

When food he fain would have.

Modernized Verse 38

Keep your weapons and tools close,

a man should not be without them.

You never know when you leave home,

what difficulties you may face.

Keywords:

Preparedness, Uncertainty

OLD VERSE 38

Away from his arms in the open field

a man should fare not a foot:

For never he knows when the need for a spear

Shall arise on the distant road.

Modernized Verse 39

No woman is too wealthy,

to appreciate being given a gift.

Even the man who has everything,

understands the kindness in a thoughtful present.

Keywords:

Graciousness

OLD VERSE 39

None so free with gifts or food have I found

That gladly he took not a gift,

Nor one who so widely,

scattered his wealth

That of recompense hatred he had.

Modernized Verse 40

Many people work very hard to acquire things,

and then forget to enjoy all that they've worked for.

Take pleasure in what you've earned,

while you're still alive to do it.

Keywords:

Thankfulness, Appreciation

OLD VERSE 40

If wealth a man has won for himself,

Let him never suffer in need;

Oft he saves for a foe what he plans for a friend,

For much goes worse than we wish.

Modernized Verse 41

With gifts, shared challenges and family bonds,

friends build stronger relationships.

Those who share in the gifts life has to offer,

may have long lasting relationships.

Keywords:

Generosity, Family Ties

OLD VERSE 41

Friends shall gladden each other with arms and garments,

As each for himself can see;

Gift-givers' friendships are longest found,

If fair their fates may be.

Modernized Verse 42

A man should be faithful to his friends,

and exchange kindness and gifts.

Laugh and have a good time with him,

but if he lies to you, don't feel ashamed to lie in return.

Keywords:

Reciprocity, Pragmatism

OLD VERSE 42

To his friend a man a friend shall prove,

And gifts with gifts requite:

But men shall mocking with mockery answer,

And fraud with falsehood meet.

Modernized Verse 43

A man should be faithful to his friends,

and the friends of his friends.

But a man should never be,

a friend to the enemy of his friends.

Keywords:

Loyalty, Fidelity

OLD VERSE 43

To his friend a man a friend shall prove,

To him and the friend of his friend;

But never a man shall friendship make

With one of his foeman's friends.

Modernized Verse 44

If you have a friend,

and know her to be loyal,

share your thoughts with her.

Exchange gifts and visit her often.

Keywords:

Friendship, Confidante

OLD VERSE 44

If a friend thou hast whom thou fully wilt trust,

And good from him wouldst get,

Thy thoughts with his mingle,

and gifts shalt thou make,

And fare to find him oft.

Modernized Verse 45

If you know someone,

but don't trust them,

and you still need something from them,

don't feel ashamed about lying and saying nice things to them.

Trade lie for lie with them,

and do what you have to do to survive.

Keywords:

Practicality, Ruthlessness

OLD VERSE 45

If another thou hast whom thou hardly wilt trust,

Yet good from him wouldst get,

Thou shalt speak him fair,

but falsely think,

And fraud with falsehood requite.

Modernized Verse 46

If a man you don't trust,

is apparently speaking his mind to you,

laugh with him, and agree with him if you must.

But keep your true thoughts to yourself.

And if he is deceiving you,

pay him back in kind.

Keywords:

Deception, Ruthlessness, Survival

OLD VERSE 46

So is it with him whom thou hardly wilt trust,

And whose mind thou mayst not know;

Laugh with him mayst thou,

but speak not thy mind,

Like gifts to his shalt thou give.

Modernized Verse 47

When I was a young man,

I traveled alone and lost my way.

I felt so relieved when I met another man on the trail.

Men feel much better in each other's company

than they do alone.

Keywords:

Companionship

OLD VERSE 47

Young was I once,

and wandered alone,

And nought of the road I knew;

Rich did I feel when a comrade I found,

For man is man's delight

Modernized Verse 48

The generous and brave person leads a good life,

seldom are they sad.

Cowards who are suspicious of everything,

and miserly with their money,

lead miserable lives,

despite what they may think.

Keywords:

Generosity, Courage

OLD VERSE 48

The lives of the brave and noble are best,
Sorrows they seldom feed;
But the coward fear of all things feels,
And not gladly the niggard gives.

Modernized Verse 49

I was walking near a field,

and I put my clothes on a pair of scarecrows.

These sticks now looked like men!

An amazing transformation with a few garments.

Men can seem more than they are,

once clothed.

Keywords:

Appearances

OLD VERSE 49

My garments once in a field I gave,

To a pair of carven poles:

heroes they seemed when clothes they had,

But the naked man is nought.

Modernized Verse 50

Like a young fir tree standing,

alone on a dreary hill,

sheltered neither by bark, needles, or other trees.

That is what it's like to be alone.

Without love and friendship,

man has little reason to be.

Keywords:

Loneliness, Companionship

OLD VERSE 50

On the hillside drear the fir-tree dies,

All bootless its needles and bark;

It is like a man whom no one loves,

-- Why should his life be long?

Modernized Verse 51

A false friendship can seem very intense in the beginning,

for perhaps a week things are wonderful,

but these relationships usually end very quickly.

By the second week there isn't much left,

and soon the friendship is sour.

Keywords:

False Friends

OLD VERSE 51

hotter than fire between false friends

Does friendship five days burn:

When the sixth day comes the fire cools,

And ended is all the love.

Modernized Verse 52

Gifts don't need to be lavish,

a small gesture can mean a lot.

Sharing a simple meal and a modest bottle of mead,

has cemented many a friendship.

Keywords:

Gift-Giving, Bonding

OLD VERSE 52

No great thing needs a man to give,

Oft little will purchase praise;

With half a loaf and a half-filled cup

A friend full fast I made.

Modernized Verse 53

A small sea hasn't much sand,

similarly, men have small minds.

Not all men are equal,

but most are still small minded.

Keywords:

Limited, Unequal, Small Minded

OLD VERSE 53

A little sand has a little sea,

And small are the minds of men;

Though all men are not equal in wisdom,

Yet half—wise only are all.

Modernized Verse 54

Man should be somewhat knowledgeable,

but never too smart.

For the best life is had,

by those who know only what they need to.

Keywords:

Middle-Wise , Content

OLD VERSE 54

A measure of wisdom each man shall have,

But never too much let him know;

The fairest lives do those men live

Whose wisdom wide has grown.

Modernized Verse 55

Man should be somewhat knowledgeable,

but never too smart.

For the intelligent often live in sadness,

the greater the wisdom, the heavier the heart.

Keywords:

Over-Wise, Despair

OLD VERSE 55

A measure of wisdom each man shall have,

But never too much let him know;

For the wise man's heart is seldom happy,

If wisdom too great he has won.

Modernized Verse 56

Man should be somewhat knowledgeable,

but never too smart.

A man that doesn't know his future ahead of time,

will sleep much better at night.

Keywords:

Hope

OLD VERSE 56

A measure of wisdom each man shall have,

But never too much let him know;

Let no man the fate before him see,

For so is he freest from sorrow.

Modernized Verse 57

A match lights a match, fire lights a candle,

and so men influence each other.

Men are known by what they say and do,

and the fool by what he doesn't.

Keywords:

Kindred Spirits, Influence, Legacy

OLD VERSE 57

A brand from a brand
is kindled and burned,
And fire from fire begotten;
And man by his speech is known to men,
And the stupid by their stillness.

Modernized Verse 58

Wake up early and work hard,

If you want to achieve great things.

The wolf that's lying down rarely gets his prey,

nor does the sleeping man achieve victory.

Keywords:

Effort, Harvest, Results

OLD VERSE 58

he must early go forth who fain the blood

Or the goods of another would get;

The wolf that lies idle shall win little meat,

Or the sleeping man success.

Modernized Verse 59

Rise early if you have few employees or resources,
and complete your own work.
Much opportunity is lost by those who sleep in,
half your wealth is won by gaining the initiative.

Keywords:

Industriousness, Initiative

OLD VERSE 59

he must early go forth
whose workers are few,
himself his work to seek;
Much remains undone for the morning–sleeper,
For the swift is wealth half won

Modernized Verse 60

It's important for men to know how to plan,

how much wood to keep you warm in the winter,

how much money to save for emergencies.

Keywords:

Planning, Contingency

OLD VERSE 60

Of seasoned shingles and strips of bark
For the thatch let one know his need,
And how much of wood he must have for a month,
Or in half a year he will use.

Modernized Verse 61

Keep a neat and tidy appearance when you go out,

but don't obsess over what you wear.

Never be ashamed of modest cloths and shoes,

or even less of an older car.

Keywords:

Pride

OLD VERSE 61

Washed and fed to the council fare,

But care not too much for thy clothes;

Let none be ashamed of his shoes and hose,

Less still of the steed he rides,

Though poor be the horse he has.

Modernized Verse 62

Like a desperate and hungry eagle,

snapping at anything that moves as he hunts over the empty sea

Make friend and cultivate allies,

or you will be that eagle,

and when you get into trouble,

you'll find yourself desperate and alone.

Keywords:

Desperation, Alliances

OLD VERSE 62

When the eagle comes to the ancient sea,

he snaps and hangs his head;

So is a man in the midst of a throng,

Who few to speak for him finds.

Modernized Verse 63

Most men have something intelligent to say,

and enjoy sharing what they know.

Tell one person your thoughts,

but be careful telling a second.

If you tell a third,

then everyone knows your business.

Keywords:

Conversation, Secrets

OLD VERSE 63

To question and answer must all be ready,

Who wish to be known as wise:

Tell one thy thoughts,

but beware of two,

All know what is known to three.

Modernized Verse 64

A prudent man exercises his strength carefully,

is mild, and is never overly forceful.

When in a room with other powerful men,

you may find you're not the top dog.

Keywords:

Restraint, Awareness

OLD VERSE 64

The man who is prudent a measured use,

Of the might he has will make;

he finds when among the brave he fares,

That the boldest he may not be.

Modernized Verse 65

Everyone should be watchful of what they say,

be slow to put your faith in a friend.

Too often something said to one person,

can harm another.

Keywords:

Measured Speech, Prudence

OLD VERSE 65

Oft for the words that to others one speaks
he will get but an evil gift.

Modernized Verse 66

I came to one feast too late,

to another one too early.

The beer was either drunk,

or not yet brewed,

a man who everyone despises is rarely welcomed.

Keywords:

Disfavor

OLD VERSE

Too early to many a meeting I came,
And some too late have I sought;
The beer was all drunk, or not yet brewed;
Little the loathed man finds.

Modernized Verse 67

You'll find yourself much more welcome,

in the homes of those where you give more than you take.

Do more for your friends than they do for you,

and you'll always find you're a welcome guest.

Keywords:

Generosity, Welcome

OLD VERSE

To their homes men would bid me hither and yon,

If at meal-time I needed no meat,

Or would hang two hams in my true friend's house,

Where only one I had eaten.

Maxims for Men

Modernized Verse 68

People should appreciate the simple things in life,

a warm fire and the golden rays of the sun.

Good health should be treasured,

and living a life without shame.

Keywords:

Simplicity, Appreciation

OLD VERSE

Fire for men is the fairest gift,

And power to see the sun; health as well,

if a man may have it,

And a life not stained with sin.

Modernized Verse 69

A woman still has worth,

even though she might have poor health.

Some are blessed with sons and daughters,

others by friends,

some by wealth,

and others by deeds they've done.

Keywords:

Worth, Relativity

OLD VERSE

All wretched is no man,

though never so sick;

Some from their sons have joy,

Some win it from kinsmen,

and some from their wealth,

And some from worthy works.

Modernized Verse 70

Better to be alive than dead,

alive you can achieve things and gain wealth.

The living can still enjoy the basic things in life,

such as a warm fire,

while the dead enjoy nothing.

Keywords:

Life, Appreciation

OLD VERSE

It is better to live than to lie a corpse,

The live man catches the cow;

I saw flames rise for the rich man's pyre,

And before his door he lay dead.

Modernized Verse 71

A crippled man can still drive a car,

the one-armed man can be a crossing guard.

Even a blind man is better than one cremated.

a dead man has no use whatsoever.

Keywords:

Life, Usefulness

OLD VERSE

The lame rides a horse,

the handless is herdsman,

The deaf in battle is bold:

The blind man is better than one that is burned,

No good can come of a corpse.

Modernized Verse 72

Having children is good.

even if it's after you've died.

Monuments and tributes are seldom seen,

unless created by your family,

for the family.

Keywords:

Legacy, Posterity

OLD VERSE

A son is better,

though late he be born,

And his father to death have fared;

Memory-stones seldom stand by the road,

Save when kinsman honors his kin.

Modernized Verse 73

Two defeat one,

your mouth can get you into trouble,

always expect danger from men.

Keywords:

Force, Prudence, Caution

OLD VERSE

Two make a battle,

the tongue slays the head;

In each furry coat a fist I look for.

Modernized Verse 74

Change can be joyful if you're prepared,

but remember that it is often still hard work.

Conditions change quickly in the short term,

and even more so in the long term.

Keywords:

Change, Effort, Expectations

OLD VERSE

he welcomes the night whose fare is enough,

Short are the yards of a ship,

Uneasy are autumn nights;

Full oft does the weather change in a week,

And more in a month's time.

Modernized Verse 75

The ignorant don't realize,

that many men become savages over wealth.

Some people are wealthy,

others are not,

there is no shame in being poor.

Keywords:

Wealth, Greed, Poverty, Appreciation

OLD VERSE

A man knows not,
if nothing he knows,
That gold oft apes begets:
One man is wealthy and one is poor,
Yet scorn for him none should know.

Modernized Verse 76

Everything and everyone dies,

you too will one day die.

But I know one thing that never dies,

fame and a good reputation for one who has earned it.

Keywords:

Fame, Reputation

OLD VERSE

Cattle die, and kinsmen die,

And so one dies one's self;

But a noble name will never die,

If good renown one gets.

Modernized Verse 77

Everything and everyone dies,

you too will one day die.

I know one thing you can't escape,

that you will be judged when you die.[5]

Keywords:

Reputation, Legacy

OLD VERSE

Cattle die, and kinsmen die,

And so one dies one's self;

One thing now that never dies,

The fame of a dead man's deeds

---

[5] This is not being judged in the Christian sense, as in by God, but rather that what you do in life will affect the opinion people have of you long after you are dead. Your name and reputation will be judged by others.

Modernized Verse 78

Once a family had plenty of money,

now they're begging in the street.

In the blink of an eye it can all be gone,

wealth is not a reliable friend.

Keywords:

Money, Unreliable, Fleeting

OLD VERSE

Among Fitjung's[6] sons saw I well-stocked folds,

Now bear they the beggar's staff;

Wealth is as swift as a winking eye,

Of friends the falsest it is.

---

[6] Fitjung's sons is a nickname for the men of Middlearth - mankind in general.

Modernized Verse 79

If you have questions, ask the runes,

which were made by mighty powers,

then stained red by Odin:

then keep silent about what is revealed.

Keywords:

Runes, Secretive

OLD VERSE

Certain is that which is sought from runes,
That the gods so great have made,
And the Master–Poet painted;
of the race of gods:
Silence is safest and best.

Modernized Verse 80

The fool become arrogant,

when he becomes wealthy,

or wins a woman's love.

His never gets wiser,

just more arrogant.

Keywords:

Arrogance

OLD VERSE

An unwise man,
if a maiden's love or wealth he chances to win,
his pride will wax,
but his wisdom never,
Straight forward he fares in conceit.

Modernized Verse 81

Praise the day once evening has come,

a tool after it has proven useful,

a good meal after it's been eaten,

and ice, once you have safely crossed it.

Keywords:

Cautious Praise

OLD VERSE

Give praise to the day at evening,

to a woman on her pyre,

To a weapon which is tried,

to a maid at wed lock,

To ice when it is crossed,

to ale that is drunk.

Modernized Verse 82

Fell trees on windy days,

row out to sea in calm weather,

have affairs in the dark, away from prying eyes in daylight.

Look for speed in a ship,

good cover from a shield.

Pick a sword for fighting,

and a girl for kissing

Keywords:

Timing, Use, Application

OLD VERSE

When the gale blows hew wood,

in fair winds seek the water;

Sport with maidens at dusk,

for day's eyes are many;

From the ship seek swiftness,

from the shield protection,

Cuts from the sword,

from the maiden kisses.

Modernized Verse 83

Drink ale by the fire, and skate on the ice,

buy a rusty car, and a skinny dog.

Fix the car yourself, and fatten up the dog.

Keywords:

Sense, Frugality

OLD VERSE

By the fire drink ale,
over ice go on skates;
Buy a steed that is lean,
and a sword when tarnished,
The horse at home fatten,
the hound in thy dwelling.

Modernized Verse 84

Men shouldn't trust the words of a girl,

or a woman's chatter,

for their fickle hearts where shaped on spinning wheel,

and lies lurk within them.

Keywords:

Fickle

OLD VERSE

A man shall trust not the oath of a maid,

Nor the word a woman speaks;

For their hearts on a whirling wheel were fashioned,

And fickle their breasts were formed.

Modernized Verse 85

A dirty gun,

a raging fire,

a starving pack of dogs,

a grunting boar,

 a croaking crow,

a boiling kettle,

a stormy sea,

a rootless tree.

Keywords:

Dangerous

OLD VERSE

In a breaking bow or a burning flame,

A ravening wolf or a croaking raven,

In a grunting boar,

a tree with roots broken,

In billowy seas or a bubbling kettle,

Modernized Verse 86

A flying bullet,

a crashing wave,

ice one day old,

a coiled snake.

Keywords:

Perilous

OLD VERSE

In a flying arrow or falling waters,
In ice new formed or the serpent's folds,
In a bride's bed-speech or a broken sword,
In the sport of bears or in sons of kings,

Modernized Verse 87

A sputtering car engine,

a sneaky employee,

a lawyers smooth words,

a check until it's cashed.

Keywords:

Apprehension

OLD VERSE

In a calf that is sick
or a stubborn thrall,
A flattering witch or a foe new slain.

Modernized Verse 88

Your brother's murderer, if you meet him,

a half-burnt house,

a car that's too fast - worthless if you crash.

Don't be so trusting as to put your faith in any of these things.

Keywords:

Distrust

OLD VERSE

In a brother's slayer, if thou meet him abroad,

In a half-burned house,

in a horse full swift

One leg is hurt and the horse is useless.

None had ever such faith as to trust in them all.

Modernized Verse 89

Don't rely on an early harvest,

or your son when he's young,

Weather can ruin your crops,

and impulsiveness rules the child.

Each of these has risks.

Keywords:

Risk, Uncertainty

OLD VERSE

hope not too surely for early harvest,

Nor trust too soon in thy son;

The field needs good weather,

the son needs wisdom,

And oft is either denied

Modernized Verse 103[7]

Be happy in your home,

cheerful with your guests, yet stay shrewd:

You should try to be thoughtful and eloquent when speaking,

if you want to be wise, and be known as such.

You may be branded a fool,

if you can't carry on an intelligent conversation,

the fool usually has nothing worth saying.

Keywords:

Caution, Speak Intelligently

OLD VERSE

Though glad at home, and merry with guests,

A man shall be wary and wise;

The sage and shrewd, wide wisdom seeking,

Must see that his speech be fair;

A fool is he named who nought can say,

For such is the way of the witless.

---

[7] Moved to this section. This verse seems to me to be a re-hash of a few of the previous messages.

Lessons for Lovers

Modernized Verse 90

The love of a fickle woman,

is like driving in snow with summer tires on your car,

or careening down the highway with no steering wheel,

or a man with a broken leg scrambling down slippery rocks.

Keywords:

Precarious

OLD VERSE

The love of women fickle of will

Is like starting o'er ice with a steed unshod,

A two-year-old restive and little tamed,

Or steering a rudderless ship in a storm,

Or, lame, hunting reindeer on slippery rocks.

Modernized Verse 91

Listen to me now,

for both of these things I know well:

Men are unfaithful to women.

Our hearts are most false when we're speaking sweet words,

but our thoughts are deceitful.

Keywords:

Deceit

OLD VERSE

Clear now will I speak,

for I know them both,

Men false to women are found;

When fairest we speak,

then falsest we think,

Against wisdom we work with deceit.

Modernized Verse 92

If a man hopes to win a woman's heart

he must learn to speak tenderly,

and make sure he can offer her wealth and security.

Tell her how beautiful she is,

learn to woo a woman, and you will win her.

Keywords:

Seduction

OLD VERSE

Soft words shall he speak

and wealth shall he offer

Who longs for a maiden's love,

And the beauty praise of the maiden bright:

he wins whose wooing is best.

Modernized Verse 93

Never laugh at another man,

for falling in love.

The lure of a beautiful woman,

often traps the wise man,

while the fool remains free.

Keywords:

Power of Love

OLD VERSE

Fault for loving let no man find,

Ever with any other;

Oft the wise are fettered,

where fools go free,

By beauty that breeds desire.

Modernized Verse 94

Don't blame a man,

for something that happens to so many.

The wisest men,

are often made into witless fools,

by the power of love.

Keywords:

Power of Love

OLD VERSE

Fault with another let no man find,

For what touches many a man;

Wise men oft into witless fools are made by mighty love.

Modernized Verse 95

You are the only one,

who knows your own heart;

For the wise,

there is no sickness worse,

 than discontent.

Keywords:

Discontent

OLD VERSE

The head alone knows what dwells near the heart,

A man knows his mind alone;

No sickness is worse to one who is wise

Than to lack the longed—for joy.

Svipdagr and Menglöð hug (1908) by W. G. Collingwood

Odin's Love Quests

Modernized Verse 96

I sat concealed in the bushes,

hoping my love would notice me.

I wanted her body and soul,

yet so concealed, I never won her love.

Keywords:

Dare or Gain Nothing

OLD VERSE

This found I myself,

when I sat in the reeds,

And long my love awaited;

As my life the maiden wise I loved,

Yet her I never had.

Modernized Verse 97

I discovered Billing's daughter on her bed,

more beautiful than sunlight sleeping.

A king's crown I would refuse,

if it meant living without her love.

Keywords:

Passion

OLÐ VERSE

Billing's daughter I found on her bed,
In slumber bright as the sun;
Empty appeared an earl's estate
Without that form so fair.

Modernized Verse 98

Come back after dark Odin,

if you wish to seduce me.

It would be disgraceful,

if anyone but us knew.

Keywords:

Affairs, Discretion

OLD VERSE

"Othin, again at evening come,
If a woman thou wouldst win:
Evil it were if others than we
Should know of such a sin."

Modernized Verse 99

Back I went to win her love,

allowing myself to be deceived.

I did not think, drunk with lust,

hoping to have my way with her.

Keywords:

Intoxication

OLD VERSE

Away I hastened, hoping for joy,

And careless of counsel wise;

Well I believed that soon I should win

Measureless joy with the maid.

Modernized Verse 100

The next night I went to her,

and discovered her surrounded by guards,

alert, with flashlights blazing.

I did not have my way with her.

Keywords:

Frustration

OLD VERSE

So came I next when night it was,

The warriors all were awake:

With burning lights and waving brands

I learned my luckess way.

Modernized Verse 101

Near morning, I once again tried to go to her.

Everyone was sound asleep;

When I got to her room,

I found she had tied a barking dog to her bed!

Keywords:

Confounded

OLD VERSE

At morning then,
when once more I came,
And all were sleeping still,
A dog found in the fair one's place,
Bound there upon her bed.

Modernized Verse 102

Many young women are found to be fickle,

though they might speak sweetly to you.

I discovered this when I lusted after a smart young lass.

The clever girl made a fool of me,

and I never laid a hand upon her.

Keywords:

Fruitless

OLD VERSE

Many fair maids,
if a man but tries them,
False to a lover are found;
That did I learn when I longed to gain
With wiles the maiden wise;
Foul scorn was my mead from the crafty maid,
And nought from the woman I won.

Odin's Quest for the Mead of Poetry

Modernized Verse 104

I sought that old Giant,

and am now safely back home,

silence wouldn't have helped me there.

but by whispering many soft speeches,

I won my desire in Suttungr's[8] halls.

Keywords:

Seduction

OLD VERSE

I found the old giant,

now back have I fared,

Small gain from silence I got;

Full many a word, my will to get,

I spoke in Suttungr's hall.

---

[8] Suttungr hid the Mead of Poetry in the center of a mountain, with his daughter, Gunnlöð, standing guard whom he turned into a witch in order to guard it. Odin eventually decided to obtain the mead. He worked for Baugi, Suttungr's brother, a farmer, for an entire summer, then asked for a small sip of the mead. Baugi drilled into the mountain and Odin changed into a snake and slithered inside. Inside, Gunnlöð was on guard but he persuaded her to give him three sips in exchange for three nights of sex. Odin proceeded to drink all the mead, changed into an eagle and escaped.

Modernized Verse 105

With an auger,

I bored a hole in the mountain,

and made room to pass through the rock;

The paths of the Giants stretched over and under me,

I dared my life for a drink of the mead.

Keywords:

Resourcefulness, Risk, Reward

OLD VERSE

The mouth of Rati
made room for my passage,
And space in the stone he gnawed;
Above and below the giants' paths lay,
So rashly I risked my head.

Modernized Verse 106

Gunnlöð gave me a drink of the glorious mead,

as I sat upon a golden stool.

I paid her for it poorly,

and left her with a broken heart.

Keywords:

Success, Treachery

OLD VERSE

Gunnloth gave on a golden stool
A drink of the marvelous mead:
A harsh reward
did I let her have for her heroic heart,
And her spirit troubled sore.

Modernized Verse 107

Gunnlöð beauty I well enjoyed,

rarely does the wily man leave unsatisfied.

Now "The Mead of Poetry"[9] has been brought up,

to the realm of the gods and shared with men.

Keywords:

Guile, Reward

OLD VERSE

The well-earned beauty well I enjoyed,

Little the wise man lacks;

So Othrörir now has up been brought

To the midst of the men of earth.

---

[9] Óðrœrir is a synonym for the mead of poetry.

Modernized Verse 108

I would not have left the Giant's home alive,

had it not been for sweet Gunnlöð,

whom I held in my arms.

Keywords:

Regret

OLD VERSE

hardly, methinks,

would I home have come,

And left the giants' land,

had not Gunnloth helped me,

the maiden good,

Whose arms about me had been.

Modernized Verse 109

The next day, the frost-giants came,

and entered the high ones hall:

they asked whether Bölverkr [10] was back among the gods,

or had Suttungr slain him below?

Keywords:

Revenge

OLD VERSE

The day that followed,

the frost-giants came,

Some word of hor to win,

And into the hall of hor;

Of Bolverk they asked,

were he back midst the gods,

Or had Suttung slain him there?

---

[10] Bölverkr was a byname for Odin, which meant "Bale Worker".

Modernized Verse 110

On his ring Odin swore an oath I thought,

how can we now trust his word?

He swindled Suttungr and stole the mead,

he beguiled Gunnloth and broke her heart.

Keywords:

Betrayal, Necessity

OLD VERSE

On his ring swore Othin,
the oath, methinks;
Who now his troth shall trust?
Suttung's betrayal he sought with drink,
And Gunnloth to grief he left.

Counseling of the Stray Singer

T he next section is addressed to someone named **Loddfafnir**. Some translate this to mean 'Stray-singer', while Carolyne Larrington renders it as 'Ragged-dragon'.

"...the name is unknown from other sources. *Lodd-* seems to mean 'rags', while Fafnir is the name of the dragon Sigurd killed. The combination 'Ragged-dragon' may be a mocking term for someone who is not yet fully initiated into arcane knowledge" (Larrington, 1999)

Regardless of who this Stray-Singer was, the verses that follow are more excellent maxims that reflect the challenges of the time.

Modernized Verse 111

It is time to chant from the chanter's stool;

I stood by the well of Urd,

I saw, and was silent, I saw, and thought,

and heard the speech of Har[11]:

I heard about what lay in the runes,

and there was much advice given.

At the hall of Har, In the hall of Har;

Such was the speech I heard.

Keywords:

Observe, Witness

OLD VERSE

It is time to chant from the chanter's stool:
By the wells of Urth I was,
I saw and was silent, I saw and thought,
And heard the speech of hor.
Of runes heard I words, nor were counsels wanting,
At the hall of hor, In the hall of hor:
Such was the speech I heard.)

---

[11] Har was another byname of Odin

Modernized Verse 112

Listen to me Loddfafnir,

and pay attention to what I have to say,

it's advice you will surely use.

Do not get up at night,

except to spy[12],

be ready for an enemy,

or to relieve yourself.

Keywords:

Security, Risk

OLD VERSE

I rede thee, Loddfafnir!
and hear thou my rede.
Profit thou hast if thou hearest,
Great thy gain if thou learnest:
Rise not at night, save if news thou seekest,
Or fain to the outhouse wouldst fare.

---

[12] Spying and readiness for an enemy is reflected in several trasnslations.

Modernized Verse 113

Listen to me Loddfafnir,

and pay attention to what I have to say,

it's advice you will surely use.

Never sleep in the arms of a woman skilled in the black arts,

such that she locks her limbs with yours.

Keywords:

Temptation

OLD VERSE

I rede thee, Loddfafnir!
and hear thou my rede,
Profit thou hast if thou hearest,
Great thy gain if thou learnest:
Beware of sleep on a witch's bosom,
Nor let her limbs ensnare thee.

Modernized Verse 114

She will cast a powerful spell on you,

and you will no longer want the advice or company of others.

Gone is your appetite for food,

and you will slumber sadly in your bed.

Keywords:

Consequences, Bereft

OLD VERSE

Such is her might that thou hast no mind

For the council or meeting of men;

Meat thou hatest,

joy thou hast not,

And sadly to slumber thou farest.

Modernized Verse 115

Listen to me Loddfafnir,

and pay attention to what I have to say,

it's advice you will surely use.

Never try to steal another man's wife.

Keywords:

Infidelity

OLD VERSE

I rede thee, Loddfafnir!
and hear thou my rede.
Profit thou hast if thou hearest,
Great thy gain if thou learnest:
Seek never to win the wife of another,
Or long for her secret love.

Modernized Verse 116

Listen to me Loddfafnir,

and pay attention to what I have to say,

it's advice you will surely use.

If you are planning a long journey,

ensure you have enough food.

Keywords:

Planning

OLD VERSE

I rede thee, Loddfafnir!

and hear thou my rede,

Profit thou hast if thou hearest,

Great thy gain if thou learnest:

If o'er mountains or gulfs thou fain wouldst go,

Look well to thy food for the way.

Modernized Verse 117

Listen to me Loddfafnir,

and pay attention to what I have to say,

it's advice you will surely use.

Never tell your troubles to an enemy,

you will get no sympathy,

and will only expose your weaknesses.

Keywords:

Guarded

OLÐ VERSE

I rede thee, Loddfafnir!
and hear thou my rede,
Profit thou hast if thou hearest,
Great thy gain if thou learnest:
An evil man thou must not let
Bring aught of ill to thee;
For an evil man will never make
Reward for a worthy thought.

Modernized Verse 118

I saw a man deeply wounded,

by a wicked woman's words.

Her lies lead to his death,

but her accusations were unjust.

Keywords:

Slander, Consequences

OLD VERSE

I saw a man who was wounded sore,

By an evil woman's word;

A lying tongue his death—blow launched,

And no word of truth there was.

Modernized Verse 119

Listen to me Loddfafnir,

and pay attention to what I have to say,

it's advice you will surely use.

If you find a faithful friend,

visit him often.

Shrubs and grass soon cover the un-trodden path.

Keywords:

Relationships, Nurturing

OLD VERSE

I rede thee, Loddfafnir!

and hear thou my rede.

Profit thou hast if thou hearest,

Great thy gain if thou learnest:

If a friend thou hast whom thou fully wilt trust,

Then fare to find him oft;

For brambles grow and waving grass

On the rarely trodden road.

Modernized Verse 120

Listen to me Loddfafnir,

and pay attention to what I have to say,

it's advice you will surely use.

Find a good man to have as a friend,

nurture the relationship,

and you will have someone to help you for life.

Keywords:

Friendship, Trust, Intimacy

OLD VERSE

I rede thee, Loddfafnir!
and hear thou my rede,
Profit thou hast if thou hearest,
Great thy gain if thou learnest:
A good man find to hold in friendship,
And give heed to his healing charms.

Modernized Verse 121

Listen to me Loddfafnir,

and pay attention to what I have to say,

it's advice you will surely use.

Never be the first to forsake a friend.

Sorrow will gnaw at your heart,

if you have no friend to confide in and unburden yourself.

Keywords:

Faithfulness, Confidante

OLD VERSE

I rede thee, Loddfafnir!

and hear thou my rede,

Profit thou hast if thou hearest,

Great thy gain if thou learnest:

Be never the first to break with thy friend

The bond that holds you both;

Care eats the heart if thou canst not speak

To another all thy thought.

Modernized Verse 122

Listen to me Loddfafnir,

and pay attention to what I have to say,

it's advice you will surely use.

Don't waste your time arguing with a fool.

Keywords:

Futility

OLD VERSE

I rede thee, Loddfafnir!
and hear thou my rede,
Profit thou hast if thou hearest,
Great thy gain if thou learnest:
Exchange of words with a witless ape
Thou must not ever make.

Modernized Verse 123

You won't get any good,

from an evil person.

A good person may help,

get you the love and respect of others.

Keywords:

Relationships, Selectiveness

OLD VERSE

For never thou mayst from an evil man

A good requital get:

But a good man oft the greatest love

Through words of praise will win thee.

Modernized Verse 124

When you can speak honestly to each other,

that is true friendship.

A friend isn't a friend,

if he only tells you what you want to hear,

sometimes a friend needs to tell you the hard truth.

Keywords:

Tough Love, Honesty

OLD VERSE

Mingled is love when a man can speak
To another all his thought;
Nought is so bad as false to be,
No friend speaks only fair.

Modernized Verse 125

Listen to me Loddfafnir,

and pay attention to what I have to say,

it's advice you will surely use.

Don't waste even three words with a lesser man.

Often the better man gets into trouble,

while the lesser man causes him harm.

Keywords:

Self-Control, Unforeseen Danger

OLD VERSE

I rede thee, Loddfafnir!

and hear thou my rede,

Profit thou hast if thou hearest,

Great thy gain if thou learnest:

With a worse man speak not three words in dispute,

Ill fares the better oft

When the worse man wields a sword.

Modernized Verse 126

Listen to me Loddfafnir,

and pay attention to what I have to say,

it's advice you will surely use.

Take great care if you make shoes,

or a roof for someone else's home.

If the shoes fit poorly,

or the roof leaks,

you will be held accountable..

Keywords:

Accountability, Responsibility

OLD VERSE

I rede thee, Loddfafnir! and hear thou my rede,—
Profit thou hast if thou hearest,
Great thy gain if thou learnest:
A shoemaker be, or a maker of shafts,
For only thy single self;
If the shoe is ill made, or the shaft prove false,
Then evil of thee men think.

Modernized Verse 127

Listen to me Loddfafnir,

and pay attention to what I have to say,

it's advice you will surely use.

If you know of someone who is evil,

say so.

Never befriend your enemies.

Keywords:

Courage, Will

OLD VERSE

I rede thee, Loddfafnir!
and hear thou my rede,
Profit thou hast if thou hearest,
Great thy gain if thou learnest:
If evil thou knowest,
as evil proclaim it,
And make no friendship with foes.

Modernized Verse 128

Listen to me Loddfafnir,

and pay attention to what I have to say,

it's advice you will surely use.

Never participate in evil,

always try to do good.

Keywords:

Hope, Goodness

OLD VERSE

I rede thee, Loddfafnir! and hear thou my rede,

Profit thou hast if thou hearest,

Great thy gain if thou learnest:

In evil never joy shalt thou know,

But glad the good shall make thee.

Modernized Verse 129

Listen to me Loddfafnir,

and pay attention to what I have to say,

it's advice you will surely use.

Dont' worry about what lay ahead on the battlefield,

Focus on the man beside you,

otherwise fear may paralyze you,

like deer caught in the head-lights.

Keywords:

Bravery, Focus, Steadfastness

OLD VERSE

I rede thee, Loddfafnir! and hear thou my rede,

Profit thou hast if thou hearest,

Great thy gain if thou learnest:

Look not up when the battle is on.

Like madmen the sons of men become,

Lest men bewitch thy wits.

Modernized Verse 130

Listen to me Loddfafnir,

and pay attention to what I have to say,

it's advice you will surely use.

If you want the love of a good woman,

speak kindly and honestly to her.

Be faithful and treat her well,

and she will return in kind.

Keywords:

Love, Tenderness, Fidelity

OLD VERSE

I rede thee, Loddfafnir! and hear thou my rede,

Profit thou hast if thou hearest,

Great thy gain if thou learnest:

If thou fain wouldst win a woman's love,

And gladness get from her,

Fair be thy promise and well fulfilled;

None loathes what good he gets.

Modernized Verse 131

Listen to me Loddfafnir,

and pay attention to what I have to say,

it's advice you will surely use.

Take care, but don't be paranoid.

Be especially careful when drinking,

or flirting with another man's wife.

Also, watch out for con men.

Keywords:

Common Sense, Balance, Guarded

OLD VERSE

I rede thee, Loddfafnir! and hear thou my rede

Profit thou hast if thou hearest,

Great thy gain if thou learnest:

I bid thee be wary,

but be not fearful;

Beware most with ale or another's wife,

And third beware lest a thief outwit thee.

Modernized Verse 132

Listen to me Loddfafnir,

and pay attention to what I have to say,

it's advice you will surely use.

Never mock, or make fun of,

a guest or traveler.

Keywords:

Respect, Guests, Travelers

OLD VERSE

I rede thee, Loddfafnir! and hear thou my rede,
Profit thou hast if thou hearest,
Great thy gain if thou learnest:
Scorn or mocking ne'er shalt thou make
Of a guest or a journey-goer.

Modernized Verse 133

You never know who is related to whom,

when at a gathering or party.

No man is blameless or has no faults,

and nobody is so evil,

he isn't worthy in some small way.

Keywords:

Awareness, Worth

OLD VERSE

Oft scarcely he knows who sits in the house

What kind is the man who comes;

None so good is found that faults he has not,

Nor so wicked

that nought he is worth.

Modernized Verse 134

Listen to me Loddfafnir,

and pay attention to what I have to say,

it's advice you will surely use.

Never laugh at the old folk,

the old often have much to teach us.

Wisdom often comes with wrinkled skin,

faded paint, and a rusted roof.

Keywords:

Respect, Age, Wisdom

OLD VERSE

I rede thee, Loddfafnir! and hear thou my rede,

Profit thou hast if thou hearest,

Great thy gain if thou learnest:

Scorn not ever the gray-haired singer,

Oft do the old speak good;

Oft from shrivelled skin come skillful counsels,

Though it hang with the hides,

And flap with the pelts, And is blown with the bellies.

Modernized Verse 135

Listen to me Loddfafnir,

and pay attention to what I have to say,

it's advice you will surely use.

Never abuse a guest, or throw them out.

Instead, help a person in need.

Keywords:

Hospitality, Kindness

OLD VERSE

I rede thee, Loddfafnir! and hear thou my rede,

Profit thou hast if thou hearest,

Great thy gain if thou learnest:

Curse not thy guest,

nor show him thy gate,

Deal well with a man in want.

Modernized Verse 136

Set your standards high,

for those you allow to enter your hall.

Remember to be generous to them,

otherwise you will be in for all sorts of grief.

Keywords:

Care, Leadership, Generosity

OLD VERSE

Strong is the beam that raised must be

To give an entrance to all;

Give it a ring,

or grim will be

The wish it would work on thee.

Modernized Verse 137

Listen to me Loddfafnir,

and pay attention to what I have to say,

it's advice you will surely use.

When you drink beer, call on the strength of the earth, for earth is good against drunkenness,

but fire is used against diseases.

Oak is good for constipation,

grain against wizardry,

bearded rye against feuds.

They say the moon is good against hate.

Alum use for rabies, and runes against evil.

The earth draws off floods.

OLD VERSE

I rede thee, Loddfafnir! and hear thou my rede,

Profit thou hast if thou hearest,

Great thy gain if thou learnest:

When ale thou drinkest seek might of earth, (For earth cures drink, and fire cures ills,

The oak cures tightness, the ear cures magic,

Rye cures rupture, the moon cures rage,

Grass cures the scab, and runes the sword—cut;)

The field absorbs the flood.

A Viking Book of Spells

In addition to a book of practical advice, the Havamal also contains the mythic "Rune Song" of Odin, which describes his acquisition of the Runes, and outlines seventeen magical spells – the eighteenth is hidden.

In the Poem, the runes or other logistical aspects of the spells are not explicitly mentioned, and so it's left to the reader to puzzle out. In Freya Aswynn's book *"Northern Mysteries & Magick – Runes & Feminine Powers"*, she giver her insight into what runes may have been associated with each spell, and goes on to describe some of the logistics involved. Freya is probably the most knowledgeable woman on the esoteric and mystical aspects of the runes alive today. Her books and CD's are a must have for any serious student, and I rely on her expertise when referring to these aspects.

For each of the spells mentioned in the rune song, I have listed three runes that Freya mentions in her book; in cases where she mentions runes beyond the three, I don't list those. You should buy her book for detailed explanations as to why she chose each of those runes, as well as other pertinent information – well worth a read!

Freya Aswynn: "Northern Mysteries and Magick: Runes & Feminine Powers"

ISBN: 978-1567180473

Please Refer to **"Appendix A: List of Runes"** for a List of the Runes used for the interpretations of the Rune Songs.

"Odin's Self-sacrifice" (1908) by W. G. Collingwood.

Modernized Verse 138

Now Odin's words will be spoken in the hall,

valuable for the sons of men,

yet deadly for the kin of giants;

Hail to Odin, and to those who learn!

He who learns these lessons will profit!

Hail to those who pay attention!

OLD VERSE

Now are hor's words spoken in the hall,

Kind for the kindred of men,

Cursed for the kindred of giants:

hail to the speaker, and to him who learns!

Profit be his who has them!

hail to them who hearken!

Modernized Verse 139

I know that I hung on the windy tree,

for nine full nights;

Wounded by a spear,

and offered to Odin,

myself to myself,

on the tree that none know,

from which root it comes.

OLD VERSE

I ween that I hung on the windy tree,

hung there for nights full nine;

With the spear I was wounded,

and offered I was To Othin,

myself to myself,

On the tree that none may ever know

What root beneath it runs.

Modernized Verse 140

None gave me drink,

none gave me food.

I looked down;

I took up the runes,

screaming I took them,

and down I fell.

OLD VERSE

None made me happy with loaf or horn,

And there below I looked;

I took up the runes,

shrieking I took them,

And forthwith back I fell.

Modernized Verse 141

Nine powerful spells I got,

from the son of Bolthorn,

Bestla's father;

and a drink of the precious mead,

poured from the cup Óðrœrir.

OLD VERSE

Nine mighty songs I got
from the son Of Bolthorn,
Bestla's father;
And a drink I got of the goodly mead
Poured out from Othrörir.

Modernized Verse 142

Then I began to thrive,

and grow wiser,

my knowledge and vitality grew,

each achievement led to another.

OLD VERSE

Then began I to thrive,

and wisdom to get,

I grew and well I was;

Each word led me on to another word,

Each deed to another deed.

Modernized Verse 143

Runes you'll find, and important predictions,

that the king of magic stained,

and the mighty gods have made;

Very powerful signs, very useful signs,

that the ruler of the gods carved.

OLD VERSE

Runes shalt thou find, and fateful signs,

That the king of singers colored,

And the mighty gods have made;

Full strong the signs,

full mighty the signs

That the ruler of gods doth write.

Modernized Verse 144

Odin for the gods,

Dain[13] for the elves,

and Dvalin[14] for the dwarves,

Alsvith for the giants,

and some I wrote myself.

OLD VERSE

Othin for the gods,
Dain for the elves,
And Dvalin for the dwarfs,
Alsvith for giants and all mankind,
And some myself I wrote.

---

[13] Dáinn, an elf who introduced the runes to his race according to Hávamál
[14] Dvalin is said to have introduced the writing of runes to the dwarves, as Dain had done for the elves and Odin for the gods.

Modernized Verse 145

Do you know how to carve them?

Do you know how to interpret them?

Do you know how to stain them?

Do you know how to test?

Do you know how to ask them?

Do you know how to sacrifice them?

Do you know how to send them?

Do you know how to use them?

OLD VERSE

Knowest how one shall write,
knowest how one shall rede?
Knowest how one shall tint,
knowest how one makes trial?
Knowest how one shall ask,
knowest how one shall offer?
Knowest how one shall send,
knowest how one shall sacrifice?

Modernized Verse 146

Better to ask for too little,

than offer too much,

the reward will be comparable to the gift.

Better not to sacrifice than to over sacrifice.

That is how Thund[15] of old carved it,

before the race of men began.

Where he rose on high,

and came home again.

OLD VERSE

Better no prayer than too big an offering,

By thy getting measure thy gift;

Better is none than too big a sacrifice,

So Thund of old wrote ere man's race began,

Where he rose on high when home he came.

---

[15] A byname for Odin.

Modernized Verse 147

I know these spells,

which are unknown to all men,

not even to kings and queens or CEO:

The first is Help;

which will bring you help with all your troubles,

and in times of sadness and stress.

OLD VERSE

The songs I know that king's wives know not,

Nor men that are sons of men;

The first is called help,

and help it can bring thee

In sorrow and pain and sickness.

Modernized Verse 148

A second I know,

which a man should chant,

if he wanted to heal the sick.

OLD VERSE

A second I know,
that men shall need
Who leechcraft long to use;

Modernized Verse 149

A third I know:

If I'm in need of protection from enemies;

when I chant this spell,

it will blunt their blades, and slow their bullets,

none of their weapons will hurt me.

OLD VERSE

A third I know,

if great is my need

Of fetters to hold my foe;

Blunt do I make mine enemy's blade,

Nor bites his sword or staff.

Modernized Verse 150

A fourth I know:

If someone binds my joints or limbs,

when I chant this spell it will set me free,

it will release the fetters from my hands and feet.

OLD VERSE

A fourth I know,
if men shall fasten
Bonds on my bended legs:
So great is the charm that forth I may go,
The fetters spring from my feet,
Broken the bonds from my hands.

Modernized Verse 151

A fifth I know:

when I see an enemy throw a rock or spear,

it will never be fast enough that I can't stop it,

as long as I get a glimpse of it.

OLD VERSE

A fifth I know,

if I see from afar

An arrow fly 'gainst the folk;

It flies not so swift that I stop it not,

If ever my eyes behold it.

Modernized Verse 152

A sixth I know;

if an enemy seeks to harm me,

his wrath will be turned back against him,

and I will remain unharmed.

OLÐ VERSE

A sixth I know,
if harm one seeks
With a sapling's roots to send me;
The hero himself who wreaks his hate
Shall taste the ill ere I.

Modernized Verse 153

A seventh I know;

if I see a building in flames,

no matter how big or hot the fire,

I know the spell to chant.

OLD VERSE

A seventh I know,

if I see in flames

The hall o'er my comrades' heads;

It burns not so wide that I will not quench it,

I know that song to sing.

Modernized Verse 154

An eighth I know;

whenever hatred flares up among my friends,

I can calm them all quickly.

OLD VERSE

An eighth I know,

that is to all

Of greatest good to learn;

When hatred grows among heroes' sons,

I soon can set it right.

Modernized Verse 155

A ninth I know;

when my ship is in danger at sea,

I can calm the winds,

and smooth the waves.

OLD VERSE

A ninth I know,
if need there comes
To shelter my ship on the flood;
The wind I calm upon the waves,
And the sea I put to sleep.

Modernized Verse 156

A tenth I know;

when I see ghosts and demons in the sky at night,

I can force them to flee,

confuse them,

and deprive them of their shape.

OLD VERSE

A tenth I know,

what time I see house-riders flying on high;

So can I work that wildly they go,

Showing their true shapes,

hence to their own homes.

Modernized Verse 157

An eleventh I know;

when I lead friends into danger,

I chant behind their shields,

bravely and safely they enter the battle,

uninjured they return home.

OLD VERSE

An eleventh I know,
if needs I must lead
To the fight my long—loved friends:
I sing in the shields, and in strength they go
Whole to the field of fight, Whole from the field of fight,
And whole they come thence home.

Modernized Verse 158

A twelfth I know;

if I see a corpse hanging on a tree,

I can carve and stain the runes,

that will return him,

and allow him to speak to me.

OLD VERSE

A twelfth I know,

if high on a tree I see a hanged man swing:

So do I write and color the runes

That forth he fares,

And to me talks.

Modernized Verse 159

A thirteenth I know;

if I sprinkle a young warrior with water,

never will he fall,

regardless of the danger,

bullets and blades will not harm him.

OLD VERSE

A thirteenth I know,
if a thane full young
With water I sprinkle well;
he shall not fall,
though he fares mid the host,
Nor sink beneath the swords.

Modernized Verse 160

A fourteenth I know;

if I speak to our folk about the gods and high ones,

I can teach them about the Ases, Elves and Dwarves,

not many know such things.

OLD VERSE

A fourteenth I know,
if fain I would name
To men the mighty gods;
All know I well of the gods and elves,
Few be the fools know this.

Modernized Verse 161

A fifteenth I know;

that before the doors of Delling[16],sang Thjodrerrir the dwarf;

Power he sent to the gods, glory for the elves,

and wisdom for Odin the wise.

OLD VERSE

A fifteenth I know,

that before the doors Of Delling

sang Thjothrörir the dwarf;

Might he sang for the gods, and glory for elves,

And wisdom for hroptatyr[17] wise.

---

[16] The Doors of Delling refer to Sunrise
[17] Hroptatyr is another byname for Odin

Modernized Verse 162

A sixteenth I know;

if I want to seduce a young woman,

I know a spell to change her mind,

and make her lust after me.

OLD VERSE

A sixteenth I know,

if I seek delight

To win from a maiden wise:

The mind I turn of the white-armed maid,

And thus change all her thoughts.

Modernized Verse 163

A seventeenth I know;

so that rarely will a young woman turn away from me,

and when I have her,

she will hardly ever look at another man.

OLD VERSE

A seventeenth I know,
so that seldom shall go
A maiden young from me;

Modernized Verse 164

An eighteenth I know;

that I would never tell to a woman young or old,

The most powerful is that which only you know.

So come the end of the spells,

the last of which remains secret,

except perhaps to one who lies in my arms, or my sister.

OLD VERSE

An eighteenth I know,

that ne'er will I tell To maiden or wife of man,

The best is what none but one's self doth know,

So comes the end of the songs, Save only to her in whose arms I lie,

Or who else my sister is.

Modernized Verse 165

Now have Odin's spells been told, in Odin's hall,

that men need,

and giants can't use.

Hail to the one who speaks them!

Hail to one who knows them!

These are useful to you who learn them,

and Hail to he who heeds these lessons!

OLÐ VERSE

Long these songs thou shalt, Loddfafnir,

Seek in vain to sing;

Yet good it were if thou mightest get them,

Well, if thou wouldst them learn,

help, if thou hadst them.

Appendix A

LIST OF RUNES

The Elder FUTHARK

ᚠ	Fehu	ᚺ	Hagalaz	↑	Teiwaz
ᚢ	Uruz	ᚾ	Nauthiz	ᛒ	Berkana
ᚦ	Thurisaz	ᛁ	Isa	ᛗ	Ehwaz
ᚨ	Ansuz	ᛃ	Jera	ᛗ	Manaz
ᚱ	Raido	ᛇ	Eihwaz	ᛚ	Laguz
ᚲ	Kenaz	ᛈ	Pertho	◊	Inguz
ᚷ	Gebo	ᛉ	Algiz	ᛞ	Dagaz
ᚹ	Wunjo	ᛋ	Sowulo	ᛟ	Othila

Page intentionally blank

Index

1

1066, 3

A

Abandonment, 54
Accomplishment, 37
Accountability, 43, 161
Affairs, 132
Age, 169
Akira Kurosawa, 1
Alcohol, 41, 43
Alertness, 34, 36
Alliances, 91
Alsvith, 181
Alum, 172
American, 20, 213
Appearances, 78
Application, 112

Appreciation, 69, 98, 100, 105
Apprehension, 117
armour, 21
Arrogance, 110
Ases, 197
Ask, 20
Aswynn, 173
Awareness, 30, 64, 93, 168

B

Bad Advice, 38
Balance, 166
battle, 21, 26, 44, 45, 101, 103, 164, 194
Bellows, 8, 27, 213
Bereft, 149
Bestla, 178
Betrayal, 144
Bhagavad-Gita, 4
Black Belt, 2

blood-price, 11
Bo-Jutsu, 2
Bolthorn, 178
Bonding, 81
boorish, 24
Bravery, 164
Bray, 8, 28, 213
Bruce Lee, 1
brutality, 21
Buddhism, 3
Buddhist, 1

C

Canada, 3
Care, 52, 156, 171
Casual Insults, 61
Caution, 20, 30, 35, 56, 103, 120
Cautious, 22, 111
Change, 104
character, 7, 8, 11, 12, 13, 17, 20, 21, 22, 25, 48
Charity, 44
Chisholm, 8, 213
Christian, 19, 22
Christianity, 8, 18, 26
Cockiness, 59
Common Sense, 39, 40, 166
Companionship, 76, 79
Compassion, 32
Concern, 32
Confidante, 73, 156
Confounded, 135
Consequences, 61, 149, 153
constipation, 172
Content, 83
Contingency, 89
Conversation, 92
corpse, 19, 100, 101, 195
Courage, 44, 77, 162
Cowardice, 45
crime, 11
cunning, 4, 10, 13, 22

D

Dain, 181
Dangerous, 58, 115
Danish, 8
Dare, 130
Deceit, 123
Deception, 75
Delling, 198
demons, 193
Dependence, 66
Despair, 84
Desperation, 91
Discontent, 127
Discourse, 57
Discretion, 132
Disfavor, 95
Distrust, 118
dojo, 2
drink, 10, 12, 33, 41, 42, 46, 48, 113, 138, 139, 140, 144, 172, 177, 178
drunk, 12, 17, 43, 48, 95, 111, 133
Drunkenness, 40, 42
Dvalin, 181
Dwarves, 197

E

Eddas, 5, 213
Effort, 87, 104
elephants, 4
Elves, 197
Empathy, 64
England, 3, 8, 15, 18
English, 7, 8, 9, 10, 12, 17, 19, 20, 21, 24, 26
ethical, 7, 10, 19
Europe, 3, 4, 17, 19, 22
European, 20, 21
exonerated, 11

F

Faithfulness, 156
False Friends, 80
Fame, 106
Family Ties, 70
Far East, 3
Fate, 45
fetters, 186, 187
feud, 11
feudal, 10
feuds, 172
Fickle, 114
Fidelity, 72, 165
flames, 100, 190
Fleeting, 108
Focus, 164
folly, 10
food, 16
Fool, 46
Foolishness, 53
fools, 11, 125, 126, 197
Force, 103
Foresight, 60
Forgetfulness, 42
France, 3
friend, 9, 14, 15, 16, 21, 35, 59, 63, 69,
     71, 72, 73, 81, 91, 94, 96, 108, 154,
     155, 156, 159
Friendship, 73, 155
Frugality, 113
Fruitless, 136
Frustration, 134
Futility, 157

G

General Knowledge,, 34
Generosity, 70, 77, 96, 171
gentleman, 17, 22
German, 19, 20
ghosts, 193
giants, 139, 142, 143, 175, 181, 202

Gift-Giving, 81
gifts, 12, 16, 68, 70, 71, 73, 75
Gluttony, 49
gods, 8
Goodness, 163
Graciousness, 33, 68
grain, 2, 172
Greed, 105
Guarded, 152, 166
Guardedness, 56
Guests, 28, 29, 167
Guile, 54, 141

H

Harvest, 87
Havamal, 1, 7, 8, 4, 5, 7, 8, 9, 10, 11,
     13, 18, 20, 21, 22, 24, 26, 27, 28,
     173
heal, 185
Heathen, 4, 5
help, 10, 7, 14, 16, 27, 37, 54, 155, 158,
     170, 184
Henry David Thoreau, 4, 5
Highlanders, 3
Hindu, 4
Hinduism, 4
Hollander, 8, 213
Honesty, 159
Hope, 85, 119, 163
Hospitality, 31, 170

I

Iaido, 2
Iceland, 4
Icelandic, 8
Ignorance, 55
immoral, 10, 21, 25
Imperfection, 51
Independence, 65
Independent Thinking, 38
India, 3, 4, 13

Indra, 4
Industriousness, 88
Infidelity, 150
Influence, 86
Initiative, 88
Intimacy, 155
Intoxication, 133
Italian, 20

J

Japan, 1, 2, 5, 9, 10
Japanese, 1, 2, 5, 7, 9, 10, 13
Ju-Jitsu, 2
justice, 16, 20

K

Kama, 2
Kanchipuram, 3
Karate, 1, 2
Kennings, 5
kill, 19
killing, 10, 11, 19
Kindness, 170
Kindred Spirits, 86
king, 44, 131, 180, 184
Knowledgeable, 57
Koizumi Yakumo, 5
Kwaidan, 5

L

Larrington, 145, 214
Latin, 13, 19
law, 11, 18
Leadership, 171
Legacy, 86, 102, 107
Life, 100, 101
Limited, 82
Loddfafnir, 145, 147, 148, 150, 151,
    152, 154, 155, 156, 157, 160, 161,

162, 163, 164, 165, 166, 167, 169,
    170, 172, 202
Loneliness, 79
Long-Winded, 58
love, 8, 10, 20, 79, 80, 110, 122, 124,
    125, 126, 130, 131, 133, 150, 158,
    159, 165
Love, 28, 64, 129, 165
Loyalty, 72
lust, 133, 199

M

Machiavelli, 4
Machiavellian, 4
magic, 5, 25, 172, 180
McGregor, 3
mead, 12, 42, 48, 81, 136, 138, 139,
    140, 141, 144, 178
Measured Speech, 94
Middle-Wise, 83
Misplaced Trust, 53
Moderation, 20, 41, 43
Money, 108
Monks, 1
morality, 9, 26
must, 8, 10, 11, 13, 15, 16, 17, 18, 21,
    22, 23, 24

N

Necessity, 144
New Orleans, 5
New Situations, 39
Niccolò Machiavelli, 4
Norman, 10, 3
Norse, 4, 5, 10, 11, 12, 15, 22, 26
Norsemen, 24
North, 1, 3, 8, 13, 17, 19, 26, 213
North America, 3
Northern, 1, 7, 8, 9, 11, 14, 17, 18,
    20, 24
Norway, 8

Nurturing, 154

O

Oak, 172
Observe, 30, 146
Obsessing, 52
Odin, 4, 28, 42, 109, 129, 132, 137, 138, 143, 144, 146, 173, 175, 176, 181, 183, 198, 202
Óðrœrir, 141, 178
Okinawan, 2
old age, 9
Old Icelandic, 8
Optimism, 44
Otter's Bath, 5
Overconfidence, 55
Over-Wise, 84

P

Passion, 131
Patrick Lafcadio Hearn, 5, 7, 26
Perilous, 116
Philosophy, 13
pirates, 8
Planning, 89, 151
Posterity, 102
Poverty, 105
Power of Love, 125, 126
Practicality, 74
Pragmatism, 71
praise, 17, 21, 24, 38, 81, 111, 124, 158
Praise, 17, 111
Precarious, 122
Precaution, 60
predictions, 180
Preparation, 62
Preparedness, 67
Pride, 90
Priorities, 62
Promptness, 31
protection, 112, 186

Proto-Indo-European, 4
Prudence, 94, 103

Q

quarrel, 6, 10, 24

R

Reciprocity, 71
Regret, 142
Relationships, 154, 158
Relativity, 63, 99
religion, 4, 21, 22
religious, 18, 19, 21, 26
Reputation, 106, 107
Reservedness, 56
Resourcefulness, 139
Respect, 38, 167, 169
Responsibility, 161
Restraint, 93
Results, 87
Retire Early, 48
Revenge, 143
Reward, 139, 141, 152
Ridicule, 59
Risk, 119, 139, 147
Roman, 19
runes, 109, 146, 172, 173, 174, 177, 181, 195
Runes, 28, 109, 173, 174, 180
Russia, 4
Ruthlessness, 74, 75
rye, 172

S

Samurai, 1, 2, 3
Scandinavian, 18
Scotland, 3
sea, 8, 82, 91, 112, 115, 192
Secretive, 109
Secrets, 57, 92

Security, 147
seduce, 132, 199
Seduction, 124, 138
Selectiveness, 158
self-control, 12, 26, 48
Self-Control, 41, 50, 160
self-defense, 1, 2
Self-Reliance, 37, 65, 66
Sense, 113
Sensei, 2
shields, 194
Shito-Ryu, 2
Shotokan, 1
shrewd, 20, 24, 26, 120
Shy, 46
sickness, 8, 127, 184
Simplicity, 98
Singapore, 3
Slander, 153
Small Minded, 82
Social Drinking, 46, 48
society, 8, 10, 12, 20, 21, 25, 26
Solomon, 14
sorrow, 14, 85, 184
Spaniard, 20, 23
sparring, 2
Speak Intelligently, 120
Speak Sensibly, 48
spear, 8, 9, 67, 176, 188
Spencer, 14, 22
spirituality, 4
Steadfastness, 164
still, 8, 9, 12, 19, 21, 25, 26
Stonehenge, 3
Stray-singer, 145
Success, 140
suicide, 18
Sutton-Hoo, 3
Sweden, 8

T

temper, 10, 12, 48

Temptation, 148
Tenderness, 165
Thankfulness, 69
thieves, 10
Thjodrerrir, 198
Thor, 4
thought, 7, 12, 20, 21, 26
Thund, 183
Timing, 64, 112
Tokyo Imperial University, 5, 7
Tonfa, 2
Tough Love, 159
Travel, 40
Travellers, 167
Treachery, 140
tribes, 19
Trust, 155

U

Uncertainty, 67, 119
Understanding, 35, 47
Unequal, 82
Unforeseen Danger, 160
unharmed, 189
University of Aberdeen, 3
Unreliable, 108
Unwelcome, 58
Ural Mountains, 4
Use, 112
Usefulness, 101

V

vengeance, 9, 11
Vigilance, 30
Viking, 3, 173, 213
vitality, 179

W

Walden, 5
warrior, 196

water, 112, 196

waves, 192

Wealth, 39, 105, 108

weapons, 9, 24

Welcome, 96

Welcoming, 33

Whale Road, 5

will, 7, 10, 13, 15, 16, 17, 20, 21, 23, 25, 26

Will, 49, 162

winds, 112, 192

wisdom, 4, 5, 8, 14, 16, 18, 22, 35, 36, 37, 39, 40, 43, 47, 82, 83, 84, 85, 110, 119, 120, 123, 179, 198

Wisdom, 1, 22, 28, 29, 35, 38, 169

wise, 9, 11, 12, 14, 15, 20, 24, 26, 34, 35, 36, 43, 44, 47, 49, 53, 57, 60, 82, 84, 92, 120, 125, 127, 130, 133, 136, 141, 198, 199

Witness, 146

wizardry, 172

women, 18, 19, 122, 123, 136

Worldliness, 34, 47

Worry, 52

Worth, 25, 99, 168

Z

Zen, 3, 5

Page intentionally blank

Bibliography

Primary References

Aswynn, F. (2002). *Northern Mysteries & Magick*. St.Paul: Llewellyn Publications.

Bellows, H. A. (1923). *The Poetic Edda*. New York: The American-Scandinavian Foundation.

Bray, O. (1908). *The Elder or Poetic Edda (Viking Club Translation Series)* . St. Paul, MN, USA: Ams Press Inc.

Chisholm, J. A. (2005). *The Eddas: The Keys to the Mysteries of the North*. n/a: scribd.com.

Hearn, L., & Erskine, J. (1921). *Books and Habits - from the lectures of Lafcadio Hearn*. New York: Dodd, Mead and Company.

Hollander, L. M. (1986). *The Poetic Edda*. Austin, Texas, USA: University of Texas Press.

Larrington, C. (1999). *The Poetic Edda*. New York: Oxford University Press.

Secondary References

Antonsen, E. H. (2002). *Runes and Germanic linguistics*. New York: Mouton de Gruyter.

Arthur, R. G. (2002). *English-Old Norse Dictionary*. Cambridge: In parentheses Publications.

Bandle, O., Elmevik, L., & Widmark, G. (2002). *The Nordic languages: An international handbook of the history of the North Germanic Language, Volume 1*. Berlin: deGruyter.

Barney, S. A. (1985). *Word-Hoard - An Introduction to Old English Vocabulary*. New Haven: Yale University Press.

Benoist, A. d. (2004). *On Being Pagan*. Atlanta: ULTRA.

Bonweits, I. (1989). *Real Magic*. York Beach: Samuel Weiser, Inc.

Chisholm, J. A. (1994). *True Hearth - A Practical Guide to Traditional Householding*. Smithville: Runa-Raven Press.

Conway, D. (1995). *Celtic Magic*. St. Paul: Llewellyn Publications.

Coulter, J. H. (2003). *Germanic Heathenry - A Practical Guide*. 1st Books Library.

Davidson, H. E. (1990). *Gods and Myths of Northern Europe*. London: Penguin Books.

Davidson, H. E. (1999). *Myths and Symbols in Pagan Europe*. Syracuse: Syracuse University Press.

Desmond, Y. (2005). *Voluspa: Seidhr as Wyrd Consciousness*. BookSurge.

Foster, M. H., & Cummings, A. M. (1922). *Asgard Stories - Tales from Norse Mythology.* Boston: Silver, Burdett and Company.

Giles, D. J., & Ingram, R. J. (890 (1823, 1847)). *The Anglo-Saxon Chronicle.* www.gutenberg.org.

Grimes, H. Y. (2010). *Heilan Yvette Grimes.* Hollow Earth Publishing.

Guerber, H. A. (1895). *Myths of northern lands.* New York: American Book Company.

Gundarsson, K. (2007). *Elves, Wights, and Trolls - Studies Towards the Practice of Germanic Heathenry: Vol. 1.* Lincoln: iUniverse.

Gundarsson, K. (2006). *Our Troth: History and Lore (Volume 1).* BookSurge Publishing.

Hardwick, C. (1872). *Traditions, Superstitions and Folk-Lore, (Chiefly Lancashire and The North of England).* Manchester: Simpkin, Marshall & Co.

Hutton, R. (2001). *The Pagan Religions of the Ancient British Isles - Their Nature and Legacy.* Malden: Blackwell Publishers Ltd.

Jesch, J. (2001). *Ships and men in the late Viking Age: the vocabulary of runic inscriptions and Skaldic Verse.* Woodbridge: The Boydell Press.

Jones, P., & Pennick, N. (1997). *A History of Pagan Europe.* New York: Routledge.

Joseph Bosworth, D. F. (1898). *An Anglo-Saxon Dictionary.* Oxford: Clarendon Press.

Keynes, S., Godden, M., & Lapidge, M. (2004). *Anglo-Saxon England.* Cambridge: Cambridge University Press.

Kraskova, G. (2005). *Exploring the Northern Tradition - A Guide to the Gods, Lore, Rites and Celebrations From the Norse, German, and Anglo-Saxon Traditions.* Franklin Lakes: The Career Press, Inc.

Kraskova, G., & Kaldera, R. (2009). *Northern Tradition for the Solitary Practitioner - A Book of Prayer. Devotional Practice and the Nine Worlds of Spirit.* Franklin: The Career Press, Inc.

Northern Wisdom

Laozi. (6th Century BCE). *Tao Te Ching*.

Larrington, C. (1999). *The Poetic Edda*. New York: Oxford University Press.

Lindow, J. (2001). *Norse Mythology - A guide to the Gods, Heroes, Rituals and Beliefs*. New York: Oxford University Press.

Logan, F. D. (2005). *The Vikings in History*. New York: Routledge.

Looijenga, T. (2003). *Texts & contexts of the oldest Runic inscriptions*. Leiden: Brill Academic Publishers.

Machiavelli, N. (1532). *The Prince*. Florence: Antonio Blado d'Asola.

Mackenzie, W. (1895). *Gaelic Incantations Charms and Blessings of the Hebrides*. Inverness: The Northern Counties Newspaper and Printing and Publishing Company, Limited.

Musashi, M. (1645). *The Book of Five Rings (Go Rin No Sho)*.

Owen, G. R. (1996). *Rites and Religions of the Anglo-Saxons*. New York: Barnes & Noble Books.

Page, R. (1999). *Runes and runic inscriptions: collected essays on Anglo-Saxon and Viking runes*. Boydell Press.

Paxson, D. L. (2006). *Essential Asatru - Walking the Path of Norse Paganism*. New York: Citadel Press.

Paxson, D. L. (2005). *Taking Up the Runes - A Complete Guide to Using Runes in Spels, Rituals, Divination, and Magic*. San Franciso: Red Wheel/Weiser, LLC.

Pennick, N. (Boston). *Magical Alphabets: The Secrets and Significance of Ancient Scripts -- Including Runes, Greek, Ogham, Hebrew and Alchemical Alphabets*. 1992: Red Wheel / Weiser.

Pennick, N. (2002). *Practical Magic in the Northern Tradition*. Loughborough: Thoth Publications.

Pennick, N. (1992). *Rune Magic*. London: The Aquarian Press.

Peschel, L. (1999). *A Practical Guide to the Runes*. St. Paul: Llewellyn Publications.

Peterson, L. A. (1977). *Edible Wild Plants - Eastern/Central North America*. New York: Houghton Mifflin.

Pitt, R. J. (1893). *The Tragedy of the Norse Gods*. London: T. Fisher Unwin.

Plowright, S. (2006). *The Rune Primer - A Down-to-Earth Guide to the Runes*. Lulu.

Plowright, S. (2000). *True Helm - A Practical Guide to Northern Warriorship*. Petersham: MacKaos Consulting for Rune-Net Press.

Polington, S. (2002). *The English Warrior - From Earliest Times Till 1066*. Wiltshire: Anglo-Saxon Books.

Pollington, S. (2006). *Wordcraft - New English to Old English Dictionary and Thesaurus*. Norfolk: Anglo-Saxon Books.

Rossman, D. ". (2005). *The Northern Path - Norse Myths and Legends Retold....and What They Reveal*. Chapel Hill: Seven Paws Press.

Shore, T. W. (1906). *Origin of the Anglo-Saxon Race*. London: Elliot Stock.

Simpson, J. (1987). *Everday Life in the Viking Age*. New York: Dorset Press.

Sorensen, V. (1989). *The Downfall of the Gods*. Lincoln: University of Nebraska Press.

Spurkland, T. (2009). *Norwegian runes and runic inscriptions*. Rochester: Boydell Press.

Svenson, R. (2003). *Pierced by the Light: Viking Gods, Runes and 21st Century Magic*. Coalville: Flying Witch Publications.

Thomas A. Wise, M. (1884). *History of Paganism on Caledonia*. London: Trubner & Co.

Thorpe, B. (1865). *A Grammar of the Anglo-Saxon Tongue, from the Danish of Erasmus Rask*. London: Trubner & Co.

Thorpe, B. (1852). *Northern Mythology, Comprising the Popular Traditions and Superstitions of Scandinavia, Norther Germany, and The Netherlands: Volume I. Northern Mythology.* London: Edward Lumley.

Thorpe, B. (1851). *Northern Mythology, Comprising the Popular Traditions and Superstitions of Scandinavia, Norther Germany, and The Netherlands: Volume II. Scandinavian Popular Traditions and Superstitions.* London: Edward Lumley.

Thorpe, B. (1852). *Northern Mythology, Comprising the Popular Traditions and Superstitions of Scandinavia, Norther Germany, and The Netherlands: Volume III. North German and Netherlandish Popular Traditions and Superstitions.* London: Edward Lumley.

Thorpe, B. (1851). *Northern Mythology, Comprising the Principal Popular Traditions and Superstitions of Scandinavia, North Germany, and the Netherlands. Volume 1.* London: Edward Lumley.

Thorsson, E. (1984). *FUTHARK - A Handbook of Rune Magic.* York Beach: Samuel Weiser Inc.

Thorsson, E. (2005). *Northern Magic - Rune Mysteries and Shamanism.* St. Paul: Llewellyn Publications.

Thorsson, E. (1990). *Rune Might: Secret Pratices of the German Rune Magicians.* St. Paul: Llewellyn Publications.

Thorsson, E. (1990). *Runelore - A Handbook of Esoteric Runology.* York Beach: Samuel Weiser, Inc.

Thorsson, E. (1994). *The Truth About Teutonic Magic.* St. Paul: Llewellyn.

Wodening, S. (2006). *Germanic Magic - A Basic Primer on Galdor, Runes, Spa, and Herbs.* Little Elm: Miercinga Rice.

Wodening, S. (2003). *Hammer of the Gods - Anglo-Saxon Paganism in Modern Times.* Little Elm: Angleseaxisce Ealdright.

Young, J. I. (1954). *the Prose Edda.* Los Angeles: University of California Press.

Northern Lore - A Field Guide to the Northern Mind, Body, & Spirit

Winner of the Global eBook Award for Best *New Age / Non-Fiction* Book in 2011

Northern Lore is a Field Guide to the Northern Mind-Body-Spirit, and will help you re-discover the Folk-Lore & Traditions of North Western Europe, and acquaint you with modern practices inspired by that lore.

In today's exciting cosmopolitan society, we tend to discard the old in favor of the new; and while discovering new traditions is a wonderful experience, it's important to also reflect on the traditions that have shaped our culture, and see where they've taken us.

Together we'll take an incredible journey back in time, and forward, embracing a synthesis of ancestral riches, and modern sensibilities. My hope is that after reading this, you'll go and dig deeper into your history - read the Eddas, harvest some herbs, practice runic yoga and cook a viking feast!

In Northern Lore you will:

- Practice "Runic Yoga" for Health and Well Being
- Learn Ancient Herblore for Holistic Healing
- Meet your Animal Spirit Guide, or Fylgia
- Discover Lost Meaning in the Days of the Week
- Explore Modern Holidays & connections to Ancestral Festivals
- Unlock the Mysteries of the Runes
- Sample Viking and Anglo-Saxon cuisine

"This book is the single most comprehensive guide to various branches of the Northern Tradition."

- Freya Aswynn, Author of Northern Mysteries and Magick: Runes & Feminine Powers

---

Available Worldwide via Amazon

The Runes in 9 minutes

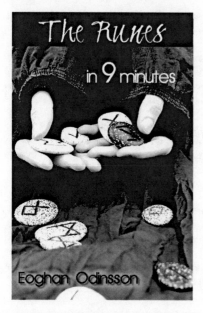

Start using the runes in 9 minutes!

In 9 minutes you will be using the runes for personal development and exploration. Of course you aren't going to master the runes in 9 minutes, but you can start!

We'll even teach you how to create your own set of runes. All you need, in addition to this book, is a sheet of paper and something to write with.

This is a book of runes for beginners, and as such, I designed it to be a concise and inexpensive introduction. If you like what you see and the runes are for you, then you can extend your studies. If the runes aren't your thing, then you haven't invested much time or money. Call it a runic sampler if you will.

In The Runes in 9 minutes you will:

- Make your own set of 24 Elder Futhark Runes
- Learn how to use the runes in 3 essential layouts
- Discover a Never Before Published way to use the runes!
- Interpret their meanings in the context of your life
- Study the symbolism of each ancient symbol
- Explore different types of runes such as the Elder Futhark, Anglo-Saxon Futhorc, and Younger Futhork
- Uncover the history and culture behind the runes

Available Worldwide via Amazon

Northern Plant Lore - A Field Guide to The Ancestral Use of Plants in Northern Europe (COMING SPRING 2012)

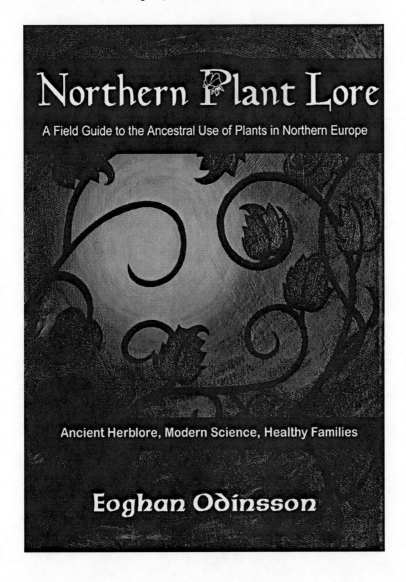

Coming Spring 2012!